GRADES 4-5
MATH BOOK

AMERICAN MATH
ACADEMY

By H. TONG, M.Ed.

Math Instructor & Olympiad Coach

www.americanmathacademy.com

MW01165875

AMERICAN MATH ACADEMY

GRADES 4-5 MATH BOOK

Writer: H.Tong
Copyright © 2023 The American Math Academy LLC.

All rights reserved. No part of this publication may be reproduced in whole or in part, stored in a retrieval system, or transmitted in any form or by any means electronic, mechanical, photocopying, recording or otherwise, without written permission of the copyright owner.

Printed in United States of America.

ISBN: 9798379105785

Although the writer has made every effort to ensure the accuracy and completeness of information contained this book, the writer assumes no responsibility for errors, inaccuracies, omissions or any inconsistency herein. Any slighting of people, places, or organizations is unintentional.

Questions, suggestions or comments, please email: americanmathacademy@gmail.com

TABLE OF CONTENTS

TABLE OF CONTENTS

TABLE OF CONTENTS

BOOKS BY AMERICA MATH ACADEMY

Kindergarten
MATH WORKBOOK
From Zero to Math Hero

From Zero to Math Hero
Second Grade Math Mastery
student's #1 Choice

GRADE 2 MATH BOOK
- 2,500+ Questions with Answers
- Covers all essential second grade math topics

From Beginner to Mastery Level

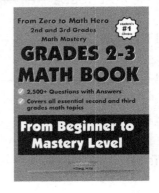

From Zero to Math Hero
2nd and 3rd Grades Math Mastery
student's #1 Choice

GRADES 2-3 MATH BOOK
- 2,500+ Questions with Answers
- Covers all essential second and third grades math topics

From Beginner to Mastery Level

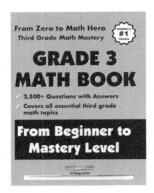

From Zero to Math Hero
Third Grade Math Mastery
student's #1 Choice

GRADE 3 MATH BOOK
- 2,500+ Questions with Answers
- Covers all essential third grade math topics

From Beginner to Mastery Level

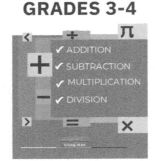

MATH WORKBOOK
GRADES 3-4
- ADDITION
- SUBTRACTION
- MULTIPLICATION
- DIVISION

From Zero to Math Hero
Third Grade Math Mastery
student's #1 Choice

GRADE 4 MATH BOOK
- 2,500+ Questions with Answers
- Covers all essential fourth grade math topics

From Beginner to Mastery Level

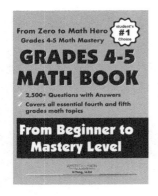

From Zero to Math Hero
Grades 4-5 Math Mastery
student's #1 Choice

GRADES 4-5 MATH BOOK
- 2,500+ Questions with Answers
- Covers all essential fourth and fifth grades math topics

From Beginner to Mastery Level

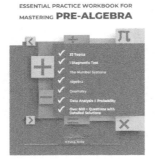

ESSENTIAL PRACTICE WORKBOOK FOR
MASTERING **PRE-ALGEBRA**

THE COMPLETE GUIDE TO
MIDDLE SCHOOL MATH
GRADES 6-8

2ᴺᴰ EDITION

ESSENTIAL PRACTICE WORKBOOK FOR
MASTERING **ALGEBRA 1**

ALGEBRA II
ESSENTIAL PRACTICE WORKBOOK
HIGH SCHOOL

ESSENTIAL WORKBOOK FOR MASTERING ALGEBRA
WORD PROBLEMS

TOPICS INCLUDE:

BOOKS BY AMERICA MATH ACADEMY

GEOMETRY
PRACTICE WORKBOOK
GRADES 7-10

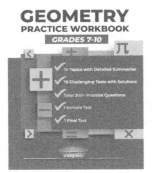

DIGITAL SAT
MATH PRACTICE BOOK

DIGITAL PSAT/NMSQT
MATH WORKBOOK

DIGITAL SAT
MATH PREP WORKBOOK

5 DIGITAL SAT
MATH PRACTICE TESTS

New ACT
MATH PRACTICE BOOK

A PREPARATION GUIDE TO
MATH COMPETITIONS

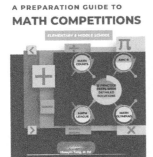

MATH OLYMPIAD
CONTESTS PREPARATION
GRADES 4-8

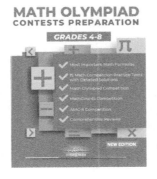

MASTERING AMC 10-12
&
OLYMPIAD CHALLENGES
GRADES 8-12

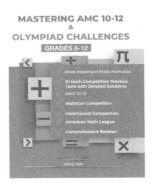

About the Author

Mr. Tong teaches at various private and public schools in both New York and New Jersey. In conjunction with his teaching, Mr. Tong developed his own private tutoring company. His company developed a unique way of ensuring their students' success on the math section of the SAT. His students, over the years, have been able to apply the knowledge and skills they learned during their tutoring sessions in college and beyond. Mr. Tong's academic accolades make him the best candidate to teach SAT Math. He received his master's degree in Math Education. He has won several national and state championships in various math competitions and has taken his team to victory in the Olympiads. He has trained students for Math Counts, American Math Competition (AMC), Harvard MIT Math Tournament, Princeton Math Contest, and the National Math League, and many other events. His teaching style ensures his students success. He personally invests energy and time into his students and sees what struggling with. His dedication towards his students is evident through his student's achievements.

Acknowledgements

I would like to take the time to acknowledge the help and support of my beloved wife, my colleagues, and my students–their feedback on my book was invaluable. I would like to say an additional thank you to my dear friend Robert for his assistance in making this book complete. Without everyone's help, this book would not be the same. I dedicate this book to my precious daughters Vera and Nora who were my inspiration to take on this project.

Pre-test

1. What digit is in hundredths place in 1.578?

A) 4

B) 6

C) 7

D) 8

2. What digit is in tenths place in 3.12?

A) 1

B) 2

C) 3

D) 5

3. What is the value of 6 in 3.046?

A) 6

B) 0.6

C) 0.06

D) 0.006

4. Which of following decimal has the greatest value?

A) 26.45

B) 26.54

C) 26.60

D) 26.46

5. Which number rounds to 35,000?

A) 33,99

B) 34,098

C) 34,890

D) 35,987

6. Round the whole number to the given place. 6,368 to the nearest thousand.

A) 4000

B) 500

C) 6000

D) 7000

American Math Academy

7. The digit 9 in 20,968 is _____ times the value of the digit 9 in 20,869.

A) 100

B) 10

C) $\frac{1}{10}$

D) $\frac{1}{100}$

8. The digit 3 in 2,638 is _____ times the value of thedigit 3 in 8,983.

A) 1

B) 10

C) 100

D) $\frac{1}{10}$

9. Which number is the product of 4.25 and 10?

A) 4.25

B) 42.5

C) 425

D) 4,250

10. Which of following expression is the same as 8×10^3?

A) 8

B) 80

C) 800

D) 8,000

11. Which of following expression is the same as 1.4×10^4?

A) 14

B) 140

C) 1,400

D) 14,000

12. Which of following expression is the same as 1.6×10^4?

A) 16

B) 160

C) 1600

D) 16,000

American Math Academy

13. Which of following expression is equivalent to 100,000?

A) 10^3

B) 10^4

C) 10^5

D) 10^6

14. Which of following can be in the blank to make the statement correct?

45,000 = 45, _____

A) ones

B) tens

C) hundreds

D) thousands

15. Which of following can be in the blank to make the statement correct?

165 = 1.65 _____

A) ones

B) tens

C) hundreds

D) thousands

16. $0.147 \times 10^3 = $ _____

A) 1.47

B) 14.7

C) 147

D) 1,470

17. 9.2 − 3.3 which of following addition problem could we use to check our answer?

A) 9.2 + 3.3

B) 3.3 + 4.3

C) 3.3 + 5.9

D) 5.9 + 5.9

18. What is 2.13 × 11?

A) 23.3

B) 23.40

C) 23.43

D) 23.45

19. What is 6.55 − 0.37?

   A) 0.0618

   B) 0.618

   C) 6.18

   D) 61.8

20. What is 37.45 + 3.28?

   A) 4.073

   B) 40.73

   C) 407.3

   D) 4,703

21. What is $0.2\overline{)16.4}$

   A) 0.82

   B) 8.2

   C) 82

   D) 820

22. What is the product of 15 and 75?

   A) 125

   B) 1,105

   C) 1,120

   D) 1,125

23. What is the sum of 567.23 and 23.6?

   A) 59.083

   B) 590.83

   C) 5,908.3

   D) 59,083

24. Find 995 ÷ 5 = ?

   A) 1.99

   B) 19.9

   C) 199

   D) 199.9

American Math Academy

25. Which fraction is **not** equivalent to $\frac{3}{4}$?

A) $\frac{9}{12}$

B) $\frac{15}{20}$

C) $\frac{5}{20}$

D) $\frac{18}{24}$

26. Find $\frac{1}{2} \div 6$

A) $\frac{1}{2}$

B) $\frac{1}{12}$

C) $\frac{1}{3}$

D) 3

27. Find $\frac{1}{5} + \frac{1}{3}$.

A) $\frac{5}{8}$

B) $\frac{8}{15}$

C) 5

D) $1\frac{7}{8}$

28. Find $\frac{1}{3} - \frac{1}{27}$.

A) $\frac{1}{27}$

B) $\frac{8}{27}$

C) 8

D) 27

29. What is the sum of 5 and $3\frac{1}{2}$?

A) $\frac{2}{17}$

B) $3\frac{1}{2}$

C) $5\frac{1}{2}$

D) $8\frac{1}{2}$

30. If Vera ate $\frac{1}{3}$ of apple and her friend Nora ate $\frac{1}{6}$ of apple. How much of the apple remains?

A) 1

B) 2

C) $\frac{1}{2}$

D) $\frac{1}{4}$

31. Find $6 \div \frac{1}{4} = ?$

A) 4

B) $\frac{2}{3}$

C) $1\frac{1}{2}$

D) 24

32. Vera and Nora were told to find the product $6 \times \frac{1}{5}$.

Vera → $6 \times \frac{1}{5} = \frac{1}{30}$

Nora → $6 \times \frac{1}{5} = \frac{6}{5}$

Which student wrote the product correctly?

A) Vera

B) Nora

C) Vera and Nora

D) None

33. The expression $\frac{3}{x-6}$ is undefined when x is equal to:

A) 3

B) 6

C) − 6

D) 0

34. Vera studied her homework $\frac{1}{5}$ hours and Nora studied her homework $\frac{2}{3}$ as long as Vera. How long did Nora study?

A) $\frac{2}{5}$

B) $\frac{3}{10}$

C) $\frac{2}{15}$

D) $\frac{9}{20}$

35. Which of the following is equal to $5(4 \times 3 - 4) + 14$?

A) 14

B) 24

C) 44

D) 54

36. Which of following algebraic equations correctly represents this sentence:

Sixty – five is four times a number, increased by nine.

A) $65 = 4x - 9$

B) $65 = 4x + 9$

C) $9 = 4x - 65$

D) $9 = 4x + 65$

American Math Academy

37. Which of the following number sentences is a correct match with the following sentence:

18 greater than the product of 3 and 4

A) $18 + 3 \times 4$

B) $18 - 3 \times 4$

C) $3 + 18 \times 4$

D) $4 + 3 \times 18$

38. Which of the following is the smallest prime number?

A) 0

B) 1

C) 2

D) 3

39. What is the least common multiple of 9 and 11?

A) 9

B) 11

C) 88

D) 99

40. What is the least common multiple of 5 and 30?

A) 5

B) 30

C) 120

D) 150

41. If x is the greatest prime factor of 21 and y is the greatest prime factor of 26, what is the value of x + y?

A) 15

B) 20

C) 25

D) 30

42. What are all the factors of 35?

A) 1, 2, 3, 5, 35

B) 0, 2, 5, 15, 35

C) 1, 5, 7, 35

D) 1, 3, 7, 35

43. Solve: $8 \times 5 - 9$.

A) 13

B) 21

C) 31

D) 41

44. Vera had $55 in her bank account. She spent $24 of her dollars. How many dollars does she have left in her bank account?

A) $31

B) $34

C) $41

D) $51

45. Which of following is the same length as 100m?

A) 0.1km

B) 1km

C) 10km

D) 100km

46. Which of following measurement of length is greatest?

A) 1m

B) 1cm

C) 100mm

D) 1km

47. _____ Liters = 5,000mL

A) 0.5

B) 5

C) 50

D) 500

48. 2 years = _____ days

A) 365

B) 730

C) 1,095

D) 1,825

49. 10 gallons = _____ quarts

A) 10

B) 20

C) 30

D) 40

American Math Academy

50. Find the volume of the figure below?

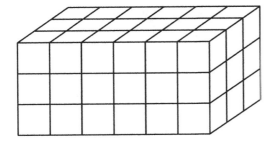

A) 9

B) 27

C) 54

D) 108

52. Find the diameter of circle below

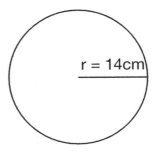

r = 14cm

A) 7cm

B) 14cm

C) 21cm

D) 28cm

51. Find the volume of the figure below?

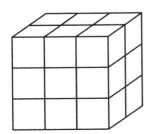

A) 6

B) 12

C) 18

D) 24

53. Find how many cube are in box below?

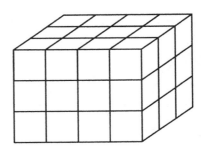

A) 6

B) 9

C) 12

D) 36

American Math Academy

54. Find the perimeter of the following shape.

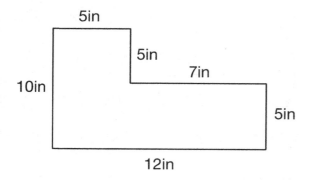

A) 17in

B) 27in

C) 44in

D) 47in

55. Find ∠ABD.

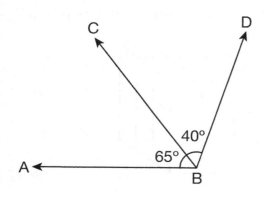

A) 90°

B) 95°

C) 100°

D) 105°

56. What are the coordinates of point A?

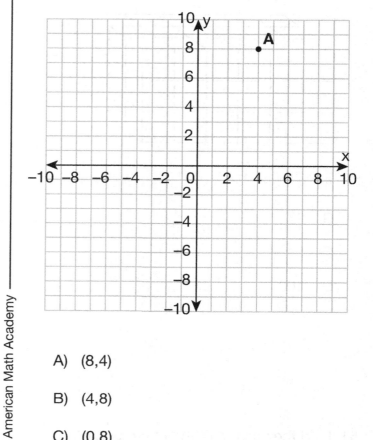

A) (8,4)

B) (4,8)

C) (0,8)

D) (4,0)

57. Which ordered pair locates a point on the y–axis?

A) (5,5)

B) (5,0)

C) (0,5)

D) (0,0)

American Math Academy

Place Value

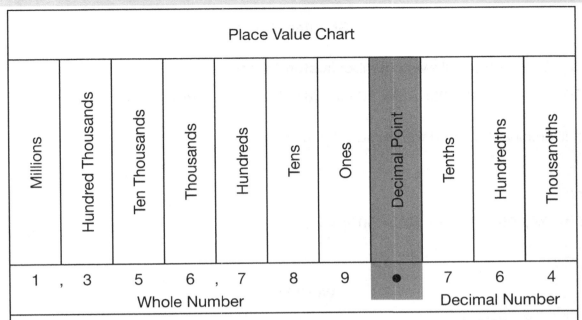

Place Value Chart

Millions	Hundred Thousands	Ten Thousands	Thousands	Hundreds	Tens	Ones	Decimal Point	Tenths	Hundredths	Thousandths
1 ,	3	5	6 ,	7	8	9	●	7	6	4

Whole Number — Decimal Number

One million, three hundred fifty six thousand, seven hundred eighty nine and 7 hundred sixty four thousandths

Expanded Form

Examples: Write each of following number in **expanded form.**

1) 35,678

2) 4,568,914

3) 145.25

Solutions:

1) 35,678: (3 × 10,000) + (5 × 1,000) + (6 × 100) + (7 × 10) + (8 × 1)

= 30,000 + 5,000 + 600 + 70 + 8

2) 4,568,914 : (4 × 1,000,000) + (5 × 100,000) + (6 × 10,000) + (8 × 1000) + (9 × 100) + (1 × 10) + (4 × 1)

= 4,000,000 + 500,000 + 60,000 + 8,000 + 900 + 10 + 4

3) 145.25 : (1 × 100) + (4 × 10) + (5 × 1) + (2 × 0.1) + (5 × 0.01)

= 100 + 40 + 5 + 0.2 + 0.05

Place Value

Standard Form

Examples: Write each of following number in **standard form.**

1) (5 × 100,000) + (7 × 10,000) + (9 × 1000) + (6 × 100) + (5 × 10) + (4 × 1)

2) Eight million,nine thousand four hundred fithy six

Solutions:

1) 500,000 + 70,000 + 9,000 + 600 + 50 + 4 = 579,654

2) 8,009,456

Word Form

Examples: Write each of following number in **word form.**

1) 4,678,459

2) 6,767

3) 123

4) 345.6

5) 0.456

Solutions:

1) 4,678,459: Four million, six hundred seventy eight, and four hundred fifty nine.

2) 6,767: Six thousand and seven hundred sixty–seven.

3) 123: One hundred twenty three.

4) 345.6:Three hundred fourth five and six tenths.

5) 0.456: Four tenths five hundredths and six thousandths.

AMERICAN MATH
ACADEMY

Expanded Form Whole Numbers Practice

Write each of following number in expanded form.

1) 9,234,456: _____

_____

2) 7,891,345: _____

_____

3) 845,612: _____

_____

4) 56,231: _____

_____

5) 6,917: _____

_____

6) 291: _____

_____

7) 31: _____

_____

8) 56,200: _____

_____

9) 6,901: _____

_____

10) 50,836: _____

_____

Expanded Form Decimal Numbers Practice

Write each of following number in expanded form.

1) 1,235.98: _____
_____

2) 485.123: _____
_____

3) 67.108: _____
_____

4) 5.145: _____
_____

5) 0.912: _____
_____

6) 0.0126 _____
_____

7) 0.9085: _____
_____

8) 1.345: _____
_____

9) 654.789: _____
_____

10) 0.0015: _____
_____

AMERICAN MATH
ACADEMY

Standard Form Whole Numbers Practice

Write each of following number in **standard form.**

1) $(6 \times 1{,}000{,}000) + (7 \times 100{,}000) + (8 \times 10{,}000) + (9 \times 1000) + (9 \times 100) + (1 \times 10) + (4 \times 1)$

_____

2) $(6 \times 100{,}000) + (6 \times 10{,}000) + (7 \times 1{,}000) + (9 \times 100) + (5 \times 10) + (2 \times 1)$

_____

3) $(9 \times 1{,}000{,}000) + (6 \times 100{,}000) + (9 \times 10{,}000) + (8 \times 1{,}000) + (7 \times 100) + (3 \times 10) + (4 \times 1)$

_____

4) $(8 \times 10{,}000) + (7 \times 1{,}000) + (9 \times 100) + (5 \times 10) + (3 \times 1)$

_____

5) $(9 \times 1000) + (4 \times 100) + (9 \times 10) + (8 \times 1)$

_____

6) $(5 \times 10{,}000{,}000) + (6 \times 1{,}000{,}000) + (4 \times 100{,}000) + (8 \times 10{,}000) + (2 \times 1{,}000)$
$+ (3 \times 100) + (4 \times 10) + (5 \times 1)$

_____

7) $(9 \times 1{,}000{,}000) + (6 \times 100{,}000) + (9 \times 10{,}000) + (8 \times 1{,}000) + (7 \times 100) + (3 \times 10) + (4 \times 1)$

_____

8) Four thousand and six hundred fourty three

_____

9) Nine hundred nineteen

_____

10) Eight thousand and four hundred sixty five

_____

11) Four hundred sixty one

_____

Standard Form Decimal Numbers Practice

Write each of following number in **standard form.**

1) (6 × 100) + (7 × 10) + (9 × 1) + (6 × 0.1) + (4 × 0.01)

_____

2) (8 × 1,000) + (3 × 100) + (7 × 10) + (4 × 1) + (5 × 0.1) + (2 × 0.01)

_____

3) (9 × 1,000,000) + (7 × 100,000) + (3 × 10,000) + (8 × 1,000) + (7 × 100) + (3 × 10) + (4 × 1)
      + (3 × 0.1) + (4 × 0.01)

_____

4) (6 × 0.0001) + (7 × 0.001) + (9 × 0.01) + (3 × 0.1)

_____

5) (1 × 100) + (2 × 10) + (3 × 1) + (8 × 0.01) + (7 × 0.1)

_____

6) (5 × 1,000,000) + (8 × 100,000) + (4 × 10,000) + (6 × 1,000) + (2 × 100) + (3 × 10) + (4 × 1)
      + (5 × 0.1) + (3 × 0.01)

_____

7) (3 × 0.0001) + (4 × 0.001) + (5 × 0.01) + (6 × 0.1)

_____

8) Nine thousand and fifty six hundredths .

_____

9) Nine hundred and thirty four hundredths .

_____

10) Seven thousand four hundred and sixty nine hundredths.

_____

11) Four thousand six hundred twenty two and three tenths.

_____

AMERICAN MATH
ACADEMY

Word Form Whole Numbers Practice

Write each of following number in **word form.**

1) 7,735,645: _____

_____

2) 785,125: _____

_____

3) 35,578: _____

_____

4) 5,974: _____

_____

5) 678: _____

_____

6) 3,000 + 300 + 30 + 3

_____

7) 4,000 + 400 + 20 + 9

_____

8) 60,000 + 7,000 + 100 + 90 + 2

_____

9) $(3 \times 100{,}000) + (6 \times 10{,}000) + (7 \times 1{,}000) + (5 \times 100) + (7 \times 10) + (4 \times 1)$

_____

10) $(3 \times 1{,}000) + (6 \times 100) + (4 \times 10) + (9 \times 1)$

_____

Word Form Decimal Numbers Practice

Write each of following number in **word form.**

1) 4,000 + 400 + 20 + 9 + 0.1:

_____

2) 60,000 + 7,000 + 100 + 90 + 2 + 0.1 + 0.01:

_____

3) 500,000 + 70,000 + 8,000 + 900 + 30 + 2 + 0.1 + 0.01:

_____

4) (4 × 100) + (6 × 10) + (5 × 1) + (6 × 0.1) + (3 × 0.01):

_____

5) (4 × 0.001) + (5 × 0.01) + (3 × 0.1):

_____

6) 8.974:

_____

7) 753.78:

_____

8) 0.008:

_____

9) 0.012:

_____

10) 0.987:

_____

AMERICAN MATH
—ACADEMY—

Compering Whole Numbers and Decimal Numbers

Compering Whole Numbers

Example: Which number is greater, 3,567 or 3,547?

Solution:

3,567
3,547
> Line up the digits.

3,5<u>6</u>7
3,5<u>4</u>7
> Compare the digits that are different.

Since, 6 is greater than 4. So, 3,567 is greater than 3,547.

3,567 > 3,547

Note:

- > That symbol means grater than.

- < That symbol means less than.

- = That symbol means equal.

Compering Decimal Numbers

Example: Which number is greater, 78.42 or78.92?

Solution:

78.42
78.92
> Line up the digits.

78.<u>4</u>2
78.<u>9</u>2
> Compare the digits that are different.

Since, 9 is greater than 4. So, 78.42 is less than 78.92.

78.42 < 78.92

Compering Whole Numbers Practice

Compare each of following pair of numbers. Write >, < or = for each.

1) 645 _____ 655

2) 1,567 _____ 1,577

3) 58 _____ 57

4) 105 _____ 115

5) 1,996 _____ 1,896

6) 2,021 _____ 2,202

7) 1,899 _____ 1,896

8) 3,200 _____ 3,202

9) 3,850 _____ 3,870

10) 5,204 _____ 5,304

11) 2,2035 _____ 2,2035

12) 2,026 _____ 2,026

13) 200,203 _____ 200,204

14) 2,220 _____ 2,201

15) 2,203 _____ 2,204

16) 2,210 _____ 2,215

17) 2,403 _____ 2,504

18) 2,980 _____ 2,890

AMERICAN MATH
ACADEMY

Compering Decimal Numbers Practice

Compare each of following pair of numbers. Write >, < or = for each.

1) 6.45 _____ 6.55

2) 1.4 _____ 2.4

3) 5.6 _____ 5.9

4) 105 _____ 105

5) 1.991 _____ 1.992

6) 2.12 _____ 2.02

7) 1.809 _____ 1.908

8) 0.123 _____ 0.120

9) 123.56 _____ 123.6

10) 0.003 _____ 0.004

11) 0.70 _____ 0.80

12) 1.4567 _____ 1.4568

13) 20.003 _____ 20.003

14) 2.025 _____ 2.201

15) 320.36 _____ 320.47

16) 0.987 _____ 0.969

17) 2.50 _____ 2.5

18) 3.60 _____ 3.05

Rounding Whole Numbers and Decimal Numbers

- Identify the units digit

- Round up or down

- If the digit is 5 or greater, add one more.

- If the digit is less than 5, leave it the same.

Example: Round 68 to the nearest tens.

Solution:

Keep the 6.

The next digit is "8" which is 5 or more, so increase the "6" by 1 to 7

The answer is 70.

Example: Round 7.85 to the nearest tenths.

Solution:

Keep the 8.

The next digit is "5" which is 5 or more, so increase the "8" by 1 to 9

The answer is 7.90

Example: Round 123 to the nearest tens.

Solution:

Keep the 2.

The next digit is "3" which is less than 5, so leave it the same.

The answer is 120.

AMERICAN MATH
ACADEMY

Rounding Whole Numbers Practice

Round each number to the place value of the underlined digit.

1) <u>6</u>,780,089

2) 34,<u>6</u>78,457

3) 503,<u>1</u>32

4) <u>7</u>,184

5) <u>2</u>,345,678

6) 3<u>7</u>5

Round each number to the place value indicated.

7) 456,346; hundreds

8) 1,234; tens

9) 3,547,892; thousands

10) 12,345,756; millions

11) 125; ones

12) 68; ones

13) 789; tens

14) 894; tens

Rounding Decimal Numbers Practice

Round each decimal to the nearest whole number.

1) 33.4

2) 36.7

3) 1.4

4) 6.8

5) 12.5

6) 34.4

Round each decimal to the nearest tenth.

7) 71.123

8) 36.403

9) 345.37

10) 56.789

11) 11.587

12) 64.48

Round each decimal to the nearest hundredth.

13) 18.687

14) 34.123

15) 5.347

16) 4.4789

Round each decimal to the nearest thousandth

17) 14.45677

18) 74.7867

19) 12.5676

20) 4.47853

21) 1.9875

22) 5.34568

AMERICAN MATH
—— ACADEMY ——

Powers of Ten

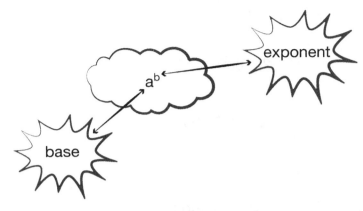

Examples: Convert following volues to a power of 10.

1) 10

2) 100

3) 1,000

4) 10,000

5) 100,000

6) 1,000,000

Solutions:

1) $10 = 10^1$

2) $100 = 10^2$

3) $1,000 = 10^3$

4) $10,000 = 10^4$

5) $100,000 = 10^5$

6) $1,000,000 = 10^6$

Examples: Convert following powers of 10 to standard numbers.

1) 10^1

2) 10^3

3) 10^5

Solutions:

1) $10^1 = 10$

2) $10^3 = 10 \times 10 \times 10$
$= 1,000$

3) $10^5 = 10 \times 10 \times 10 \times 10 \times 10$
$= 100,000$

Notes:

$10^1 = 10$ $10^2 = 100$ $10^3 = 1000$ $10^4 = 10000$

Powers of Ten Practice

Convert following volues to a power of 10.

1) 100

2) 1000

3) 10,000

4) 100,000

5) 1,000,000

6) 1,000,000,000

Convert following powers of 10 to standard numbers.

7) 10^3

8) 10^6

9) 10^7

10) 10^1

11) 10^5

12) 10^9

13) 10^4

14) 10^{10}

15) 10^{12}

Identify the base and exponent in each of the following.

16) 10^4

base:

power:

17) 10^6

base:

power:

18) 10^8

base:

power:

Write the numerals in exponential form with the given base and exponent.

19) base:10

power: 4

20) base:10

power:7

21) base: 10

power:9

AMERICAN MATH
ACADEMY

Chapter 1 Test

1. What digit is in hundredths place in 34.678?

A) 4

B) 6

C) 7

D) 8

2. What digit is in tenths place in 5.123?

A) 1

B) 2

C) 3

D) 5

3. What is the value of 5 in 23.045?

A) 5

B) 0.5

C) 0.05

D) 0.005

4. What is the value of 7 in 568.473?

A) 7

B) 0.7

C) 0.07

D) 0.007

5. Which of following decimal has the greatest value?

A) 23.45

B) 23.54

C) 23.60

D) 23.46

6. Which number rounds to 25,000?

A) 2,399

B) 24,098

C) 24,890

D) 25,987

7. Round the whole number to the given place.

48 to the nearest ten.

A) 47

B) 48

C) 49

D) 50

American Math Academy

Chapter 1 Test

8. Round the whole number to the given place.

5,368 to the nearest thousand.

A) 4,000

B) 5,000

C) 6,000

D) 7,000

9. The digit 5 in 205,678 is _____ times the value of the 5 in 256,789.

A) 100

B) 10

C) $\frac{1}{10}$

D) $\frac{1}{100}$

10. The digit 7 in 102,678 is _____ times the value of the 7 in 238,987.

A) 1

B) 10

C) 100

D) $\frac{1}{10}$

11. Which number is the product of 1.23 and 10?

A) 1.23

B) 12.3

C) 123

D) 1,230

12. Which of following expression is the same as 18×10^3?

A) 18

B) 180

C) 1,800

D) 18,000

13. Which of following expression is the same as 1.3×10^4?

A) 13

B) 130

C) 1,300

D) 13,000

AMERICAN MATH
ACADEMY

American Math Academy

14. Which of following expression is the same as 25.6×10^4?

A) 256

B) 2,560

C) 25,600

D) 256,000

17. Which of following can be in the blank to make the statement correct?

$35,000 = 35,$ _____

A) ones

B) tens

C) hundreds

D) thousands

15. Which of following expression is equivalent to 1,000,000?

A) 10^3

B) 10^4

C) 10^5

D) 10^6

18. Which of following can be in the blank to make the statement correct?

$145 = 1.45$ _____

A) ones

B) tens

C) hundreds

D) thousands

16. Which of following expression is equivalent to 1,000?

A) 10^1

B) 10^2

C) 10^3

D) 10^4

19. $0.153 \times 10^3 =$ _____

A) 1.53

B) 15.3

C) 153

D) 1,530

Adding Whole Numbers and Decimal Numbers

Adding Whole Numbers

- Line up the numbers and fill in any empty places with zeros, then add the whole numbers

Example: add 3,456 + 4,342

Solution:
```
   3,456
   4,342
+ _____
   7,798
```

Example: add 5,460 + 1,206

Solution:
```
   5,460
   1,206
+ _____
   6,666
```

Adding Decimal Numbers

- Line up the decimals and fill in any empty places with zeros, then add the decimal numbers.

Example: add 0.05 + 0.06

Solution:
```
   0.05
   0.06
+ _____
   0.11
```

Example: add 1.43 + 0.7

Solution:
```
   1.43
   0.70
+ _____
   2.13
```

Adding Whole Numbers Practice

For questions 1 through 18, add.

1) 6,356 + 5,302 = _____

2) 1,734 + 2,987 = _____

3) 12,345 + 10,302 = _____

4) 123,734 + 204,987 = _____

5) 13,000 + 5,200 = _____

6) 123,567 + 2,900 = _____

7) 125 + 3,567 = _____

8) 1,205 + 2,905 = _____

9) 14,567 + 205 = _____

10) 1,879 + 2,050 = _____

11) 1, 678
  1, 405
+ _____

12) 7, 645
  10, 208
+ _____

13) 12, 983
  13, 404
+ _____

14) 123, 809
  204, 208
+ _____

15) 105, 987
  210, 400
+ _____

16) 678, 806
  567, 208
+ _____

17) 985, 000
  134, 492
+ _____

18) 1,677, 805
  127, 203
+ _____

Adding Decimal Numbers Practice

For questions 1 through 18, add.

1) 0.07 + 0.08 = _____

2) 1.005 + 1.345 = _____

3) 12.345 + 2.34 = _____

4) 11.678 + 2.987 = _____

5) 13.08 + 5.20 = _____

6) 123.567 + 2.89 = _____

7) 12.5 + 3.47 = _____

8) 1.89 + 20.67 = _____

9) 145.6 + 123.567 = _____

10) 19.57 + 2.050 = _____

11) 1. 68
      1. 405
    + _____

12) 4. 645
      10. 20
    + _____

13) 1. 983
      0. 894
    + _____

14) 0. 0380
      2. 0027
    + _____

15) 105. 789
      545. 400
    + _____

16)   1. 806
      25. 208
    + _____

17)   3. 000
      123. 492
    + _____

18) 1. 0078
      18. 203
    + _____

AMERICAN MATH
ACADEMY

Subtracting Whole Numbers and Decimal Numbers

Subtracting Whole Numbers

- Line up the numbers and fill in any empty places with zeros, then subtract the whole numbers.

Example: Subtract 225 – 134

Solution:
$$
\begin{array}{r}
\overset{1\,12}{2\cancel{2}5} \\
-\ 134 \\
\hline
91
\end{array}
$$

Subtracting Decimal Numbers

- Line up the numbers and fill in any empty places with zeros, then subtract the decimal numbers.

Example: Subtract 12.34 – 11.54

Solution:
$$
\begin{array}{r}
\overset{1\ \,13}{12.\cancel{3}4} \\
-\ 11.54 \\
\hline
00.80
\end{array}
$$

Example: Subtract 0.05 – 0.04

Solution:
$$
\begin{array}{r}
0.05 \\
-\ 0.04 \\
\hline
0.01
\end{array}
$$

Subtracting Whole Numbers Practice

For questions 1 through 18, subtract.

1) 6,353 – 5,402 = _____

2) 1,836 – 1,582 = _____

3) 12,345 – 10,302 = _____

4) 123,734 – 112,987 = _____

5) 13,000 – 5,200 = _____

6) 6,567 – 1,900 = _____

7) 9,125 – 3,567 = _____

8) 1,995 – 1,905 = _____

9) 14,567 – 205 = _____

10) 1,879 – 1,050 = _____

11) 1, 678
    1, 405
 – _____

12) 7, 645
    6, 208
 – _____

13) 12, 983
    11, 404
 – _____

14) 123, 809
    104, 208
 – _____

15) 125, 987
    110, 400
 – _____

16) 678, 806
    567, 208
 – _____

17) 985, 000
    134, 492
 – _____

18) 1,677, 805
    127, 203
 – _____

AMERICAN MATH
—ACADEMY—

Subtracting Decimal Numbers Practice

For questions 1 through 18, subtract.

1) 0.04 – 0.03 = _____

2) 1.02 – 1.01 = _____

3) 12.37 – 2.98 = _____

4) 19.78 – 13.98 = _____

5) 13.08 – 8.30 = _____

6) 0.567 – 0.48 = _____

7) 1.5 – 0.47 = _____

8) 1.89 – 1.67 = _____

9) 145.6 – 123.567 = _____

10) 19.56 – 2.05 = _____

11) 7. 68
  – 3. 70
  _____

12) 7. 45
  – 6. 26
  _____

13) 112. 980
  – 0. 894
  _____

14) 0. 0380
  – 0. 0027
  _____

15) 105. 89
  – 45. 90
  _____

16) 67. 80
  – 25. 90
  _____

17) 4. 000
  – 3. 492
  _____

18) 9. 00
  – 8. 99
  _____

Multiplying Whole Numbers and Decimal Numbers

Multiplying Whole Numbers

- Line up the numbers up on the right.
- Start multiplying by ones digit then tens digit.
- Add the product then regroup if needed.

Example: Multiply 53 × 35 = _____

Solution:

```
      53
      35
   ×_____
     265
    1590
   +_____
    1850
```

Multiplying Decimal Numbers

- Line up the numbers up on the right.
- Multiply ignoring the decimals.
- Start multiplying by ones digit then tens digit.
- Count the decimal places in the problem.
- Move the decimal the same number of spaces to the left in the product
- Add the product then regroup if needed.

Example: Multiply 2.35 × 0.04 = _____

Solution: Line up the numbers up on the right.

2.35 → move 2 spaces rigth   235

0.04 → move 2 spaces right   4

×_____   ×_____

940 → move 4 spaces to the left side for final answer.   940

= 0.0940

Multiplying Whole Numbers Practice

For questions 1 through 18, multiply.

1) $63 \times 5 = $ _____

2) $836 \times 8 = $ _____

3) $345 \times 10 = $ _____

4) $734 \times 87 = $ _____

5) $13 \times 52 = $ _____

6) $567 \times 190 = $ _____

7) $9 \times 367 = $ _____

8) $1,995 \times 18 = $ _____

9) $144 \times 205 = $ _____

10) $178 \times 150 = $ _____

11) 678
$\times$ 405 _____

12) 45
$\times$ 28 _____

13) 983
$\times$ 40 _____

14) 809
$\times$ 78 _____

15) 125
$\times$ 400 _____

16) 806
$\times$ 208 _____

17) 1000
$\times$ 492 _____

18) 1805
$\times$ 203 _____

Multiplying Decimal Numbers Practice

For questions 1 through 18, multiply.

1) $3.1 \times 4 =$ _____

2) $8.6 \times 0.8 =$ _____

3) $3.5 \times 10 =$ _____

4) $7.4 \times 8 =$ _____

5) $12.5 \times 8 =$ _____

6) $5.7 \times 19 =$ _____

7) $9 \times 3.7 =$ _____

8) $9.5 \times 18 =$ _____

9) $44 \times 2.05 =$ _____

10) $7.8 \times 1.5 =$ _____

11) 67
$$\times \quad 4.5$$

12) 45
$$\times \quad 0.8$$

13) 8.3
$$\times \quad 4.0$$

14) 0.89
$$\times \quad 0.78$$

15) 1.25
$$\times \quad 9$$

16) 8.06
$$\times \quad 2.08$$

17) 1.87
$$\times \quad 9.2$$

18) 0.17
$$\times \quad 1.2$$

AMERICAN MATH
━ACADEMY━

Dividing Whole Numbers and Decimal Numbers

Dividing Whole Numbers

- First divide, then multiply and then subtract.

Example: Divide 963 ÷ 3 = _____

Solution:

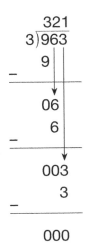

$$
\begin{array}{r}
321 \\
3\overline{)963} \\
9 \\
\hline
06 \\
6 \\
\hline
003 \\
3 \\
\hline
000
\end{array}
$$

Dividing Decimal Numbers

- Move the decimal point in the divisor.
- Move the decimal point in the dividend to the right the same number of places.
- Move the decimal point up and divide.

Example: Divide 2.48 ÷ 1.2 = _____

1.2)12.48 ⟶ Move the decimal point in the divisor.

Solution:

$$
\begin{array}{r}
10.4 \\
12\overline{)124.8} \\
12 \\
\hline
0048 \\
48 \\
\hline
00
\end{array}
$$

Dividing Whole Numbers Practice

For questions 1 through 18, divide.

1) 63 ÷ 3 = _____

2) 836 ÷ 2 = _____

3) 345 ÷ 5 = _____

4) 832 ÷ 4 = _____

5) 130 ÷ 13 = _____

6) 243 ÷ 9 = _____

7) 1000 ÷ 10 = _____

8) 995 ÷ 5 = _____

9) 144 ÷ 12 = _____

10) 625 ÷ 25 = _____

11) $3\overline{)123}$

12) $8\overline{)800}$

13) $20\overline{)640}$

14) $12\overline{)720}$

15) $32\overline{)160}$

16) $12\overline{)900}$

17) $18\overline{)540}$

18) $24\overline{)960}$

19) $50\overline{)1000}$

20) $18\overline{)378}$

AMERICAN MATH
ACADEMY

Dividing Decimal Numbers Practice

For questions 1 through 18, divide.

1) $6.4 \div 2 =$ _____

2) $8.36 \div 4 =$ _____

3) $3.45 \div 5 =$ _____

4) $8.32 \div 8 =$ _____

5) $1.20 \div 12 =$ _____

6) $25 \div 0.5 =$ _____

7) $5.45 \div 5 =$ _____

8) $9.9 \div 11 =$ _____

9) $14.4 \div 12 =$ _____

10) $60 \div 2.5 =$ _____

11) $3\overline{)12.3}$

12) $8\overline{)88.8}$

13) $2.4\overline{)48.0}$

14) $1.2\overline{)7.20}$

15) $1.2\overline{)16.8}$

16) $2.5\overline{)94.5}$

17) $1.4\overline{)4.2}$

18) $2.4\overline{)4.8}$

19) $9.2\overline{)27.6}$

20) $0.6\overline{)3.6}$

Adding and Subtracting Patterns

Example: Complete the patterns in following table.

Add 5	1	3	5	7	9	11

Solution:

Add 5	1	3	5	7	9	11
	5 + 1 = 6	5 + 3 = 8	5 + 5 = 10	5 + 7 = 12	5 + 9 = 14	5 + 11 = 16

Example: Complete the patterns in following table.

Subtract 6	13	15	17	19	21	23

Solution:

Subtract 6	13	15	17	19	21	23
	13 – 6 = 7	15 – 6 = 9	17 – 6 = 11	19 – 6 = 13	21 – 6 = 15	23 – 6 = 17

AMERICAN MATH
—ACADEMY—

Adding and Subtracting Patterns Practice

Example: Complete the patterns in each of following table.

1)

Add 7	3	6	9	12	15	18

2)

Add 12	12	22	32	42	52	62

3)

Subtract 4	5	10	15	20	25	30

4)

Subtract 6	6	12	24	36	48	60

5)

Add 11	9	18	27	36	45	54

6)

Add 25	1	3	5	7	9	11

7)

Subtract 4	10	20	30	40	50	60

8)

Subtract 9	20	35	45	55	65	75

9)

Add 15	10	23	35	47	59	61

10)

Add 16	32	37	42	47	52	57

Multiplication and Division Patterns

Example: Complete the patterns in following table.

Multiply by 7	0	5	10	15	20	25

Solution:

Multiply by 7	0	5	10	15	20	25
	7 × 0 = 0	7 × 5 = 35	7 × 10 = 70	7 × 15 = 105	7 × 20 = 140	7 × 25 = 175

Example: Complete the patterns in following table.

Divide by 10	30	40	50	60	70	80

Solution:

Divide by 10	30	40	50	60	70	80
	30 ÷ 3 = 3	40 ÷ 10 = 4	50 ÷ 10 = 5	60 ÷ 10 = 6	70 ÷ 10 = 7	80 ÷ 10 = 8

AMERICAN MATH
ACADEMY

Multiplication and Division Patterns Practice

Example: Complete the patterns in each of following table.

1)

Multiply by 3	7	8	9	10	11

2)

Multiply by 5	12	13	14	15	16

3)

Multiply by 4	15	20	25	30	35

4)

Multiply by 6	6	12	18	24	36

5)

Divide by 11	11	33	44	55	66	77

6)

Divide by 5	10	30	50	70	90	100

7)

Multiply by 8	8	10	12	14	16	18

8)

Multiply by 10	11	13	15	17	19	21

9)

Divide by 6	24	36	48	54	60	66

10)

Divide by 7	14	21	28	35	49	63

Chapter 2 Test

1. 8.2 – 4.3 which of following addition problem could we use to check our answer?

   A) 8.2 + 4.2

   B) 4.2 + 4.3

   C) 4.2 + 3.9

   D) 4.3 + 3.9

2. What is 6.12 × 12?

   A) 7.344

   B) 73.44

   C) 734.4

   D) 7,344

3. What is 7.35 – 0.14?

   A) 0.721

   B) 7.21

   C) 721

   D) 7,210

4. What is 34.45 + 3.18?

   A) 3.763

   B) 37.63

   C) 376.3

   D) 3,763

5. What is 7,445 + 319?

   A) 77.64

   B) 776.4

   C) 7,764

   D) 77,640

6. What is 555 – 378?

   A) 1.77

   B) 17.7

   C) 177

   D) 177.7

American Math Academy

7. What is $0.2\overline{)18.6}$

A) 0.93

B) 9.3

C) 93

D) 930

8. What is the product of 25 and 125?

A) 31.25

B) 312.5

C) 3,125

D) 30,125

9. What is the sum of 567.23 and 23.6?

A) 59.083

B) 590.83

C) 5,908.3

D) 59,083

10. Find $885 \div 5 = ?$

A) 1.77

B) 17.7

C) 177

D) 177.7

11. What is the value of expression below?

$1,237 - 1,198$

A) 0.39

B) 3.9

C) 39

D) 390

12. What is the value of expression below?

19.8×19.9

A) 3.9402

B) 39.402

C) 394.02

D) 3,940.2

Fraction and Types of Fractions

Fractions: Fractions are numbers that can be in the form $\frac{A}{B}$ where B is not equal to zero.

Examples: $\frac{1}{5}, \frac{1}{7}, \frac{1}{8}, \ldots$

Types of Fractions

Proper fractions: A fraction where the numerator is less than the denominator.

$$\left.\begin{array}{l} \frac{A}{B} \longrightarrow \text{numerator} \\ \phantom{\frac{A}{B}} \longrightarrow \text{denominator} \end{array}\right\} A < B$$

Example: $\frac{1}{3}$

Improper fractions: A fraction where the denominator is less than the numerator.

$$\left.\begin{array}{l} \frac{A}{B} \longrightarrow \text{numerator} \\ \phantom{\frac{A}{B}} \longrightarrow \text{denominator} \end{array}\right\} A > B$$

Example: $\frac{8}{4}$

Mixed Fractions: When a fraction is written in the form $A\frac{B}{C}$

Example: $1\frac{1}{4}$

AMERICAN MATH
ACADEMY

Fraction and Types of Fractions Practice

Identify whether the following fractions are proper or improper.

1) $\frac{1}{2}$

2) $\frac{4}{5}$

3) $\frac{1}{9}$

4) $\frac{13}{9}$

5) $\frac{25}{8}$

6) $\frac{9}{10}$

7) $\frac{131}{18}$

8) $\frac{145}{205}$

9) $\frac{19}{21}$

---

10) Which of following is a proper fraction?

A) $\frac{19}{18}$

B) $\frac{13}{12}$

C) $\frac{1}{18}$

D) $\frac{4}{3}$

11) Which of following is an improper fraction?

A) $\frac{1}{8}$

B) $\frac{3}{4}$

C) $\frac{1}{2}$

D) $\frac{4}{3}$

12) Which of following is a mixed fraction?

A) $\frac{1}{6}$

B) $\frac{2}{3}$

C) $\frac{1}{5}$

D) $1\frac{1}{3}$

13) $\frac{1}{3}$ is which of following type of fraction?

A) Proper fraction

B) Improper fraction

C) Mixed fraction

D) Not a fraction

American Math Academy

Equivalent Fractions

Equivalent fraction is a fraction with the same value as another fraction. To check equivalent fraction you can multiply numerator and denominator by the same whole number.

Examples:

1) Find two equivalent fractions of $\frac{1}{3}$?

2) Find two equivalent fractions of $\frac{1}{4}$?

3) Find two equivalent fractions of $\frac{3}{7}$?

Solutions:

1) $\frac{1}{3} = \frac{1 \times 2}{3 \times 2} = \frac{2}{6}$ or $\frac{1}{3} = \frac{1 \times 3}{3 \times 3} = \frac{3}{9}$

Two equivalent fractions of $\frac{1}{3}$, it can be $\frac{2}{6}$ and $\frac{3}{9}$.

2) $\frac{1}{4} = \frac{1 \times 2}{4 \times 2} = \frac{2}{8}$ or $\frac{1}{4} = \frac{1 \times 3}{4 \times 3} = \frac{3}{12}$

Two equivalent fractions of $\frac{1}{4}$, it can be $\frac{2}{8}$ and $\frac{3}{12}$.

3) $\frac{3}{7} = \frac{3 \times 2}{7 \times 2} = \frac{6}{14}$ or $\frac{3}{7} = \frac{3 \times 3}{7 \times 3} = \frac{9}{21}$

Two equivalent fractions of $\frac{3}{7}$, it can be $\frac{6}{14}$ and $\frac{9}{21}$.

Examples:

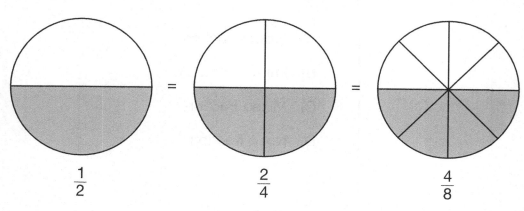

$$\frac{1}{2} \qquad \frac{2}{4} \qquad \frac{4}{8}$$

AMERICAN MATH
ACADEMY

Equivalent Fractions Practice

For questions 1 through 12, complete the equivalent fractions.

1. $\dfrac{1}{5} = \dfrac{\boxed{}}{10}$

2. $\dfrac{1}{6} = \dfrac{\boxed{}}{30}$

3. $\dfrac{1}{8} = \dfrac{\boxed{}}{80}$

4. $\dfrac{1}{7} = \dfrac{\boxed{}}{49}$

5. $\dfrac{1}{6} = \dfrac{\boxed{}}{150}$

6. $\dfrac{3}{5} = \dfrac{\boxed{}}{20}$

7. $\dfrac{5}{4} = \dfrac{\boxed{}}{40}$

8. $\dfrac{6}{7} = \dfrac{\boxed{}}{70}$

9. $\dfrac{8}{9} = \dfrac{\boxed{}}{90}$

10. $\dfrac{\boxed{}}{28} = \dfrac{1}{7}$

11. $\dfrac{18}{9} = \dfrac{6}{\boxed{}}$

12. $\dfrac{25}{150} = \dfrac{1}{\boxed{}}$

13. Which of following is equivalent to $\dfrac{1}{2}$?

A)
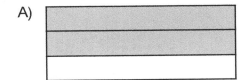

B)
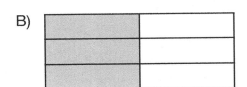

C)
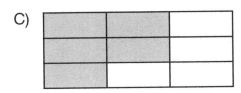

D)
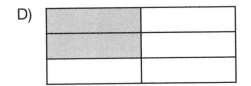

14. Which of the following fractions has the largest value?

A) $\dfrac{4}{5}$

B) $\dfrac{6}{7}$

C) $\dfrac{7}{8}$

D) $\dfrac{12}{11}$

15. Which of the following fractions is listed correctly?

A) $\dfrac{1}{2} = \dfrac{2}{3}$

B) $\dfrac{3}{2} = \dfrac{6}{18}$

C) $\dfrac{3}{2} = \dfrac{4}{9}$

D) $\dfrac{6}{5} = \dfrac{12}{10}$

American Math Academy

Compering Fractions

You can check compering fractions with following 2 methods.

- Find equivalent fractions with same denominator then compere the fractions.

Example: Write >, = or < to compare the following fractions.

$$\frac{2}{3} \ ? \ \frac{4}{5}$$

Solution:

$$\frac{2}{3} \ ? \ \frac{4}{5} \ \rightarrow \text{ Common denominators of 3 and 5 is 15.}$$

$$\frac{2 \times 5}{3 \times 5} \ ? \ \frac{4 \times 3}{5 \times 3}$$

$$\frac{10}{15} \ ? \ \frac{12}{15} \ \text{So, } \frac{10}{15} \text{ is less than } \frac{12}{15}$$

$$\frac{10}{15} < \frac{12}{15}$$

- Cross–multiplies and then compere the products.

Example: Write >, = or < to compare the following fractions.

$$\frac{1}{5} \ ? \ \frac{3}{4} \ \rightarrow \text{ Cross multiply}$$

Because of 4 is less than 15, then $\frac{1}{5}$ is less than $\frac{3}{4}$ or $\frac{1}{5} < \frac{3}{4}$

AMERICAN MATH
ACADEMY

Compering Fractions Practice

For questions 1 through 15 write >, = or < to compare the following fractions.

1) $\dfrac{1}{6}$ ———— $\dfrac{3}{7}$

2) $\dfrac{4}{5}$ ———— $\dfrac{3}{11}$

3) $\dfrac{5}{6}$ ———— $\dfrac{8}{9}$

4) $\dfrac{12}{16}$ ———— $\dfrac{13}{7}$

5) $\dfrac{9}{5}$ ———— $\dfrac{13}{8}$

6) $\dfrac{7}{9}$ ———— $\dfrac{6}{9}$

7) $\dfrac{21}{5}$ ———— $\dfrac{8}{7}$

8) $\dfrac{7}{9}$ ———— $\dfrac{4}{18}$

9) $\dfrac{42}{9}$ ———— $\dfrac{19}{4}$

10) $\dfrac{40}{6}$ ———— $\dfrac{50}{7}$

11) $\dfrac{70}{8}$ ———— $\dfrac{16}{3}$

12) $\dfrac{90}{9}$ ———— $\dfrac{40}{4}$

13) $\dfrac{10}{6}$ ———— $\dfrac{10}{7}$

14) $\dfrac{20}{5}$ ———— $\dfrac{16}{4}$

15) $\dfrac{30}{6}$ ———— $\dfrac{20}{4}$

16) Which of following fractions has the largest value?

A) $\dfrac{1}{2}$

B) $\dfrac{2}{3}$

C) $\dfrac{4}{5}$

D) $\dfrac{5}{6}$

17) Which of the following fractions is listed correctly?

A) $\dfrac{1}{2} < \dfrac{2}{3}$

B) $\dfrac{3}{2} < \dfrac{6}{7}$

C) $\dfrac{5}{4} < \dfrac{8}{9}$

D) $\dfrac{6}{5} < \dfrac{10}{9}$

18) Which of following is $\dfrac{2}{3}$?

A)

B)

C)

D)

Adding likely Fractions

Adding Fractions: When you add fractions, if they have same denominator, you add the numerators while keeping the denominator the same.

Examples:

1) $\dfrac{1}{3} + \dfrac{2}{3} = ?$

2) $\dfrac{5}{20} + \dfrac{13}{20} = ?$

3) $\dfrac{7}{17} + \dfrac{8}{17} = ?$

4) $\dfrac{45}{14} + \dfrac{20}{14} = ?$

Solutions:

1) $\dfrac{1}{3} + \dfrac{2}{3} = \dfrac{3}{3} = 1$

2) $\dfrac{5}{20} + \dfrac{13}{20} = \dfrac{5+13}{20} = \dfrac{18}{20} = \dfrac{9}{10}$

3) $\dfrac{7}{17} + \dfrac{8}{17} = \dfrac{7+8}{17} = \dfrac{15}{17}$

4) $\dfrac{45}{14} + \dfrac{20}{14} = \dfrac{45+20}{14} = \dfrac{65}{14} = 4\dfrac{8}{14} = 4\dfrac{4}{7}$

Adding likely Fractions Practice

For questions 1 through 21 add. Give the answer in simplest form.

1) $\dfrac{7}{3} + \dfrac{9}{3} = ?$

2) $\dfrac{11}{20} + \dfrac{23}{20} = ?$

3) $\dfrac{7}{19} + \dfrac{8}{19} = ?$

4) $\dfrac{1}{4} + \dfrac{2}{4} = ?$

5) $\dfrac{5}{6} + \dfrac{3}{6} = ?$

6) $\dfrac{11}{7} + \dfrac{8}{7} = ?$

7) $\dfrac{8}{11} + \dfrac{27}{11} = ?$

8) $\dfrac{5}{20} + \dfrac{13}{20} = ?$

9) $\dfrac{12}{17} + \dfrac{15}{17} = ?$

10) $\dfrac{2}{15} + \dfrac{3}{15} = ?$

11) $\dfrac{7}{30} + \dfrac{13}{30} = ?$

12) $\dfrac{1}{19} + \dfrac{3}{19} = ?$

13) $\dfrac{6}{14} + \dfrac{3}{14} = ?$

14) $\dfrac{9}{40} + \dfrac{13}{40} = ?$

15) $\dfrac{35}{17} + \dfrac{32}{17} = ?$

16) $1\dfrac{1}{2} + 1\dfrac{1}{2} = ?$

17) $2\dfrac{1}{2} + 3\dfrac{1}{2} = ?$

18) $1\dfrac{1}{6} + \dfrac{5}{6} = ?$

19) $1\dfrac{2}{3} + 1\dfrac{1}{3} = ?$

20) $4\dfrac{1}{5} + 2\dfrac{1}{5} = ?$

21) $5\dfrac{2}{7} + 1\dfrac{5}{7} = ?$

Adding unlikely Fractions

If the fractions have different denominators:

- Find the least common multiple (LCM) of both numbers.
- Rewrite the fractions as equivalent fractions with the LCM as the denominator.

Examples:

1) $\dfrac{1}{2} + \dfrac{2}{3} = ?$

2) $\dfrac{5}{20} + \dfrac{3}{5} = ?$

3) $\dfrac{3}{4} + \dfrac{2}{8} = ?$

4) $\dfrac{5}{4} + \dfrac{1}{12} = ?$

Solutions:

1) $\dfrac{1}{2} + \dfrac{2}{3} = \dfrac{1\times3}{2\times3} + \dfrac{2\times2}{3\times2} = \dfrac{3}{6} + \dfrac{4}{6} = \dfrac{7}{6} = 1\dfrac{1}{6}$

2) $\dfrac{5}{20} + \dfrac{3}{5} = \dfrac{5\times1}{20\times1} + \dfrac{3\times4}{5\times4} = \dfrac{5}{20} + \dfrac{12}{20} = \dfrac{17}{20}$

3) $\dfrac{3}{4} + \dfrac{2}{8} = \dfrac{3\times2}{4\times2} + \dfrac{2}{8} = \dfrac{8}{8} = 1$

4) $\dfrac{5}{4} + \dfrac{1}{12} = \dfrac{5\times3}{4\times3} + \dfrac{1}{12} = \dfrac{16}{12} = \dfrac{4}{3}$

AMERICAN MATH
ACADEMY

Adding unlike Fractions Practice

For questions 1 through 21 add. Give the answer in simplest form.

1) $\dfrac{2}{5} + \dfrac{1}{3} = ?$

2) $\dfrac{1}{20} + \dfrac{2}{5} = ?$

3) $\dfrac{7}{6} + \dfrac{1}{3} = ?$

4) $\dfrac{1}{2} + \dfrac{2}{4} = ?$

5) $\dfrac{5}{15} + \dfrac{3}{5} = ?$

6) $\dfrac{1}{27} + \dfrac{2}{9} = ?$

7) $\dfrac{7}{18} + \dfrac{5}{6} = ?$

8) $\dfrac{4}{20} + \dfrac{3}{4} = ?$

9) $\dfrac{1}{17} + \dfrac{1}{2} = ?$

10) $\dfrac{2}{3} + \dfrac{1}{2} = ?$

11) $\dfrac{1}{3} + \dfrac{3}{5} = ?$

12) $\dfrac{1}{9} + \dfrac{1}{3} = ?$

13) $\dfrac{3}{14} + \dfrac{1}{7} = ?$

14) $\dfrac{9}{40} + \dfrac{3}{20} = ?$

15) $\dfrac{5}{4} + \dfrac{3}{12} = ?$

16) $\dfrac{1}{5} + \dfrac{1}{2} = ?$

17) $\dfrac{5}{10} + \dfrac{4}{50} = ?$

18) $\dfrac{7}{6} + \dfrac{5}{36} = ?$

19) $1\dfrac{1}{9} + \dfrac{1}{6} = ?$

20) $1\dfrac{1}{3} + 1\dfrac{1}{4} = ?$

21) $\dfrac{2}{5} + 1\dfrac{5}{7} = ?$

Subtracting likely Fractions

Subtracting Fractions: When you subtract fractions that have the same denominators, you subtract only the numerators and keep the denominator the same.

Examples:

1) $\dfrac{5}{4} - \dfrac{1}{4} = ?$

2) $\dfrac{5}{10} - \dfrac{3}{10} = ?$

3) $\dfrac{7}{7} - \dfrac{3}{7} = ?$

4) $\dfrac{8}{9} - \dfrac{1}{9} = ?$

Solutions:

1) $\dfrac{5}{4} - \dfrac{1}{4} = \dfrac{5-1}{4} = \dfrac{4}{4} = 1$

2) $\dfrac{5}{10} - \dfrac{3}{10} = \dfrac{5-3}{10} = \dfrac{2}{10}$

3) $\dfrac{7}{7} - \dfrac{3}{7} = \dfrac{7-3}{7} = \dfrac{4}{7}$

4) $\dfrac{8}{9} - \dfrac{1}{9} = \dfrac{8-1}{9} = \dfrac{7}{9}$

Subtracting likely Fractions Practice

For questions 1 through 21 subtract. Give the answer in simplest form.

1) $\dfrac{13}{3} - \dfrac{5}{3} = ?$

2) $\dfrac{43}{30} - \dfrac{23}{30} = ?$

3) $\dfrac{50}{19} - \dfrac{18}{19} = ?$

4) $\dfrac{20}{4} - \dfrac{12}{4} = ?$

5) $\dfrac{15}{6} - \dfrac{9}{6} = ?$

6) $\dfrac{33}{7} - \dfrac{27}{7} = ?$

7) $\dfrac{51}{11} - \dfrac{47}{11} = ?$

8) $\dfrac{60}{20} - \dfrac{18}{20} = ?$

9) $\dfrac{75}{17} - \dfrac{45}{17} = ?$

10) $\dfrac{42}{15} - \dfrac{38}{15} = ?$

11) $\dfrac{77}{30} - \dfrac{53}{30} = ?$

12) $\dfrac{79}{19} - \dfrac{17}{19} = ?$

13) $\dfrac{48}{14} - \dfrac{47}{14} = ?$

14) $\dfrac{100}{40} - \dfrac{89}{40} = ?$

15) $\dfrac{19}{7} - \dfrac{12}{7} = ?$

16) $2\dfrac{1}{2} - \dfrac{1}{2} = ?$

17) $1\dfrac{5}{10} - \dfrac{4}{10} = ?$

18) $1\dfrac{1}{6} - \dfrac{5}{6} = ?$

19) $2\dfrac{1}{3} - 1\dfrac{1}{3} = ?$

20) $3\dfrac{1}{4} - 1\dfrac{1}{4} = ?$

21) $5\dfrac{1}{5} - 2\dfrac{1}{5} = ?$

Subtracting Unlikely Fractions

If the fractions have different denominators:

- Find the least common multiple (LCM) of both numbers.

- Rewrite the fractions as equivalent fractions with the LCM as the denominator.

Examples:

1) $\dfrac{1}{2} - \dfrac{1}{4} = ?$

2) $\dfrac{1}{3} - \dfrac{1}{6} = ?$

3) $\dfrac{3}{4} - \dfrac{2}{8} = ?$

4) $\dfrac{1}{4} - \dfrac{1}{20} = ?$

Solutions:

1) $\dfrac{1}{2} - \dfrac{1}{4} = \dfrac{1 \times 2}{2 \times 2} - \dfrac{1}{4} = \dfrac{2}{4} - \dfrac{1}{4} = \dfrac{2-1}{4} = \dfrac{1}{4}$

2) $\dfrac{1}{3} - \dfrac{1}{6} = \dfrac{1 \times 2}{3 \times 2} - \dfrac{1}{6} = \dfrac{2}{6} - \dfrac{1}{6} = \dfrac{1}{6}$

3) $\dfrac{3}{4} - \dfrac{2}{8} = \dfrac{3 \times 2}{4 \times 2} - \dfrac{2}{8} = \dfrac{6}{8} - \dfrac{2}{8} = \dfrac{4}{8}$

4) $\dfrac{1}{4} - \dfrac{1}{20} = \dfrac{1 \times 5}{4 \times 5} - \dfrac{1}{20} = \dfrac{5}{20} - \dfrac{1}{20} = \dfrac{4}{20} = \dfrac{1}{5}$

Subtracting unlikely Fractions Practice

For questions 1 through 21 subtract. Give the answer in simplest form.

1) $\dfrac{5}{12} - \dfrac{1}{4} = ?$

2) $\dfrac{3}{10} - \dfrac{3}{30} = ?$

3) $\dfrac{5}{19} - \dfrac{1}{38} = ?$

4) $\dfrac{7}{3} - \dfrac{1}{4} = ?$

5) $\dfrac{5}{6} - \dfrac{6}{9} = ?$

6) $\dfrac{3}{7} - \dfrac{2}{28} = ?$

7) $\dfrac{3}{11} - \dfrac{7}{33} = ?$

8) $\dfrac{1}{10} - \dfrac{3}{40} = ?$

9) $\dfrac{5}{17} - \dfrac{1}{51} = ?$

10) $\dfrac{3}{4} - \dfrac{2}{5} = ?$

11) $\dfrac{7}{3} - \dfrac{3}{2} = ?$

12) $\dfrac{9}{10} - \dfrac{17}{30} = ?$

13) $\dfrac{8}{2} - \dfrac{7}{3} = ?$

14) $\dfrac{10}{15} - \dfrac{9}{60} = ?$

15) $\dfrac{1}{7} - \dfrac{1}{8} = ?$

16) $2\dfrac{1}{2} - \dfrac{1}{3} = ?$

17) $1\dfrac{1}{4} - \dfrac{1}{3} = ?$

18) $\dfrac{5}{3} - \dfrac{11}{6} = ?$

19) $2\dfrac{1}{3} - 1\dfrac{1}{12} = ?$

20) $3\dfrac{1}{4} - 1\dfrac{1}{20} = ?$

21) $5\dfrac{1}{8} - 2\dfrac{1}{9} = ?$

Multiplying Fractions

Step by step:

- Multiply the numerators
- Multiply the denominators
- Simplify the fraction if needed

Examples:

1) $\dfrac{12}{5} \times \dfrac{3}{7} = ?$

2) $\dfrac{2}{5} \times \dfrac{3}{4} = ?$

3) $\dfrac{2}{4} \times \dfrac{3}{4} = ?$

4) $1\dfrac{2}{5} \times 1\dfrac{3}{4} = ?$

Solutions:

1) $\dfrac{12}{5} \times \dfrac{3}{7} = \dfrac{12 \times 3}{5 \times 7} = \dfrac{36}{35} = 1\dfrac{1}{35}$

2) $\dfrac{2}{5} \times \dfrac{3}{4} = \dfrac{2 \times 3}{5 \times 4} = \dfrac{6}{20} = \dfrac{3}{10}$

3) $\dfrac{2}{4} \times \dfrac{3}{4} = \dfrac{2 \times 3}{4 \times 4} = \dfrac{6}{16} = \dfrac{3}{8}$

4) $1\dfrac{2}{5} \times 1\dfrac{3}{4} = \dfrac{7}{5} \times \dfrac{7}{4} = \dfrac{49}{20} = 2\dfrac{9}{20}$

AMERICAN MATH
ACADEMY

Multiplying Fractions Practice

For questions 1 through 21 multiply. Give the answer in simplest form.

1) $\dfrac{1}{3} \times \dfrac{5}{2} = ?$

2) $\dfrac{5}{10} \times \dfrac{7}{30} = ?$

3) $\dfrac{10}{9} \times \dfrac{1}{8} = ?$

4) $\dfrac{7}{3} \times \dfrac{1}{7} = ?$

5) $\dfrac{5}{9} \times \dfrac{6}{9} = ?$

6) $\dfrac{3}{4} \times \dfrac{1}{18} = ?$

7) $\dfrac{1}{11} \times \dfrac{33}{4} = ?$

8) $\dfrac{1}{10} \times \dfrac{30}{8} = ?$

9) $\dfrac{5}{17} \times \dfrac{51}{3} = ?$

10) $\dfrac{2}{5} \times \dfrac{3}{4} = ?$

11) $\dfrac{8}{3} \times \dfrac{3}{2} = ?$

12) $\dfrac{11}{100} \times \dfrac{10}{40} = ?$

13) $1\dfrac{1}{2} \times \dfrac{7}{3} = ?$

14) $\dfrac{1}{12} \times \dfrac{3}{7} = ?$

15) $1\dfrac{1}{7} \times \dfrac{14}{8} = ?$

16) $2\dfrac{1}{2} \times \dfrac{1}{4} = ?$

17) $1\dfrac{1}{4} \times 1\dfrac{1}{3} = ?$

18) $1\dfrac{1}{6} \times \dfrac{3}{5} = ?$

19) $2\dfrac{1}{3} \times 1\dfrac{1}{7} = ?$

20) $3\dfrac{1}{4} \times 1\dfrac{1}{13} = ?$

21) $5\dfrac{1}{8} \times 2\dfrac{1}{41} = ?$

Dividing Fractions

Flip the divisor, second fraction.

Multiply the numerator–by–numerator and denominator–by–denominator.

Simplify the fraction if needed.

Examples:

1) $\dfrac{1}{9} \div \dfrac{2}{9} = ?$

2) $\dfrac{12}{5} \div \dfrac{4}{5} = ?$

3) $\dfrac{44}{4} \div \dfrac{33}{5} = ?$

4) $3\dfrac{1}{5} \div 1\dfrac{5}{4} = ?$

Solutions:

1) $\dfrac{1}{9} \div \dfrac{2}{9} = \dfrac{1}{9} \times \dfrac{9}{2} = \dfrac{9}{18} = \dfrac{1}{2}$

2) $\dfrac{12}{5} \div \dfrac{4}{5} = \dfrac{12}{5} \times \dfrac{5}{4} = \dfrac{60}{20} = \dfrac{6}{2} = 3$

3) $\dfrac{44}{4} \div \dfrac{33}{5} = \dfrac{44}{4} \times \dfrac{5}{33} = \dfrac{\overset{4}{\cancel{44}}}{4} \times \dfrac{5}{\underset{3}{\cancel{33}}} = \dfrac{4}{4} \times \dfrac{5}{3} = \dfrac{1}{1} \times \dfrac{5}{3} = \dfrac{5}{3} = 1\dfrac{2}{3}$

4) $3\dfrac{1}{5} \div 1\dfrac{5}{4} = \dfrac{16}{5} \times \dfrac{9}{4} = \dfrac{\overset{4}{\cancel{16}}}{5} \times \dfrac{9}{\underset{1}{\cancel{4}}} = \dfrac{4}{5} \times \dfrac{9}{1} = \dfrac{36}{5} = 7\dfrac{1}{5}$

AMERICAN MATH
—ACADEMY—

Dividing Fractions Practice

For questions 1 through 21 divide. Give the answer in simplest form.

1) $\dfrac{1}{5} \div \dfrac{5}{3} = ?$

2) $\dfrac{5}{10} \div \dfrac{3}{40} = ?$

3) $\dfrac{10}{9} \div \dfrac{5}{3} = ?$

4) $\dfrac{7}{3} \div \dfrac{7}{1} = ?$

5) $\dfrac{12}{25} \div \dfrac{6}{50} = ?$

6) $\dfrac{3}{4} \div \dfrac{1}{18} = ?$

7) $\dfrac{1}{11} \div \dfrac{1}{33} = ?$

8) $\dfrac{1}{10} \div \dfrac{1}{100} = ?$

9) $\dfrac{5}{8} \div \dfrac{15}{24} = ?$

10) $\dfrac{7}{4} \div \dfrac{21}{8} = ?$

11) $\dfrac{2}{3} \div \dfrac{18}{27} = ?$

12) $\dfrac{11}{100} \div \dfrac{88}{10} = ?$

13) $1\dfrac{1}{2} \div \dfrac{9}{4} = ?$

14) $\dfrac{1}{8} \div \dfrac{3}{6} = ?$

15) $1\dfrac{1}{5} \div \dfrac{4}{5} = ?$

16) $3\dfrac{1}{2} \div \dfrac{7}{2} = ?$

17) $1\dfrac{1}{8} \div 1\dfrac{1}{3} = ?$

18) $1\dfrac{1}{9} \div \dfrac{2}{5} = ?$

19) $2\dfrac{1}{4} \div 1\dfrac{1}{5} = ?$

20) $2\dfrac{1}{6} \div 3\dfrac{1}{6} = ?$

21) $4\dfrac{7}{8} \div 1\dfrac{1}{12} = ?$

Word Problems with Fractions Practice

1. A grocery store bought 45 pounds of tomatoes and sold $\frac{5}{9}$ on the same day. At the end of the day, how many pounds of tomatoes where left?

   A) 25 pounds

   B) 20 pounds

   C) 45 pounds

   D) 81 pounds

2. There are 24 students in math class. If $\frac{2}{3}$ of the students in this class are male students, find the number of female students in the math class?

   A) 6

   B) 8

   C) 12

   D) 16

3. The width of a rectangular garden is $1\frac{2}{3}$ cm. The length is $1\frac{4}{5}$ cm. Which of the following is the area of the garden?

   A) $\frac{1}{3}$ cm²

   B) 3 cm²

   C) $\frac{2}{3}$ cm²

   D) 4 cm²

4. Tony has 12 pencils and wants to give $\frac{3}{4}$ of them to a friend while keeping the rest for himself. How many pencils would his friend get?

   A) 3

   B) 6

   C) 8

   D) 9

5. Last night, Tony spent $1\frac{1}{8}$ hours doing his math homework. John did his math homework for $\frac{1}{4}$ as many hours as Tony did. How many hours did John spend on his homework?

   A) $\frac{9}{32}$

   B) $4\frac{1}{2}$

   C) $\frac{3}{8}$

   D) $\frac{3}{16}$

American Math Academy

AMERICAN MATH
ACADEMY

1. Which fraction is **not** equivalent to $\frac{3}{4}$?

A) $\frac{6}{8}$

B) $\frac{12}{16}$

C) $\frac{15}{20}$

D) $\frac{9}{8}$

4. Find $\frac{1}{2}+\frac{1}{3}$.

A) $\frac{5}{6}$

B) $1\frac{1}{5}$

C) 5

D) 6

2. Which fraction is equivalent to $\frac{1}{3}$?

A) $\frac{15}{5}$

B) $\frac{12}{15}$

C) $\frac{15}{25}$

D) $\frac{15}{45}$

5. Find $\frac{1}{3}-\frac{1}{18}$.

A) $\frac{5}{6}$

B) $\frac{5}{18}$

C) $\frac{1}{15}$

D) 0

3. Find $3\frac{1}{2} \div 7 = ?$

A) $\frac{1}{2}$

B) $1\frac{1}{2}$

C) $\frac{1}{3}$

D) $\frac{49}{2}$

6. Find $1\frac{1}{3} \times 1\frac{1}{8}$

A) $\frac{1}{4}$

B) $\frac{1}{2}$

C) $1\frac{1}{2}$

D) 4

American Math Academy

Chapter 3 Test

7. What is difference between $1\frac{3}{4}$ and $1\frac{1}{2}$?

   A) $\frac{1}{4}$

   B) $\frac{1}{2}$

   C) 2

   D) 4

8. What is sum of 5 and $3\frac{1}{2}$?

   A) $\frac{2}{17}$

   B) $3\frac{1}{2}$

   C) $5\frac{1}{2}$

   D) $8\frac{1}{2}$

9. If Vera ate $\frac{1}{4}$ of apple and her friend Nora ate $\frac{1}{2}$ of apple. How much of the apple remains?

   A) 1

   B) 2

   C) $\frac{1}{2}$

   D) $\frac{1}{4}$

10. Find $9 \div \frac{1}{4} = ?$

    A) 9

    B) $\frac{4}{9}$

    C) $2\frac{1}{4}$

    D) 36

11. What is product of $\frac{1}{3}$ and $\frac{1}{9}$?

    A) $\frac{1}{27}$

    B) 27

    C) 3

    D) $\frac{1}{3}$

12. Vera and Nora were told to find the product

$5 \times \dfrac{1}{9}$

Vera $\rightarrow 5 \times \dfrac{1}{9} = \dfrac{1}{45}$

Nora $\rightarrow 5 \times \dfrac{1}{9} = \dfrac{5}{9}$

Which student wrote the product correctly?

A) Vera

B) Nora

C) Vera and Nora

D) None

13. The expression $\dfrac{3}{x-5}$ is undefined when x is equal to:

A) 3

B) 5

C) 8

D) -5

14. Which of the following fractions has the largest value?

A) $\dfrac{4}{9}$

B) $\dfrac{1}{3}$

C) $\dfrac{8}{18}$

D) $\dfrac{10}{18}$

15. Vera studied her homework $\dfrac{3}{5}$ hours and Nora studied her homework $\dfrac{4}{3}$ as long as Vera. How long did Nora study?

A) $\dfrac{3}{5}$

B) $\dfrac{4}{5}$

C) $\dfrac{5}{4}$

D) $\dfrac{9}{20}$

Order of Operations

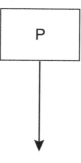

Parentheses

Do any operations in parentheses

$$36 + 4(8 - 3) - 2^3 \div 4$$
$$36 + 4 \times 5 - 2^3 \div 4$$

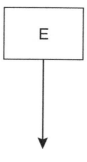

Exponents

Do any Exponents

$$36 + 4 \times 5 - 2^3 \div 4$$
$$36 + 4 \times 5 - 8 \div 4$$

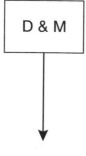

Divide and multiply rank equally (Always work, salve, or move, etc left to right)

$$36 + 4 \times 5 - 8 \div 4$$
$$36 + 20 - 2$$

Add and subtract rank equally (Always work, salve, or move, etc left to right)

$$36 + 20 - 2$$
$$56 - 2$$
$$54$$

AMERICAN MATH
ACADEMY

Order of Operations Practice

Solve the following problems with PEMDAS.

1) $2 \times 3 - 4$

2) $12 \div 3 \times 3 - 4$

3) $4 \div 2 \times 3 - 6$

4) $2 \times 3 \div 3 - 2$

5) $2(6 \div 3) - 1$

6) $(12 - 4) \div 2 \times 3 - 6$

7) $1 - 4 \times 3 \div 3 + 12$

8) $2(18 \div 3) + 1$

9) $2 \times 3 - 6(5 - 4)$

10) $2^2 - 3 \times 3 - 3 + 7$

11) $2^2 - 3 \div 3 - 3 + 8$

12) $4 \times 3 - 3(8 - 5)$

13) $12 - (2 - 4 \times 3) + 5$

14) $4 \times 2 - 3 + 8$

15) $4 \times 3 + 3(15 \div 5)$

16) $2 + 4 \times 5 - 5$

17) $5 \times 2 - 1 + 8$

18) $3 \times 12 - 18 \div 6$

19) $(4 \times 5 - 5) \div 5$

20) $18 \times 2 \div 12 - 3$

21) $60 \div 12 - 8$

22) $4(2 \times 5 - 5)$

23) $(9 \times 2) \div (12 - 3)$

24) $(60 - 10) \div 5 \times 4 - 8$

Prime and Composite Numbers

Prime Numbers	Composite Numbers
A number that has only two factors, 1 and itself. 2, 3, 5, 7, 11, 13, 17, ...	A number that has more than two factors 4, 6, 8, 10, 12, 14, ...

0 and 1 are neither

Prime and Composite Numbers Practice

1. Circle the numbers that are prime numbers:

1	2	3	4	5
6	7	8	9	10
11	12	13	14	15
16	17	18	19	20
21	22	23	24	25

2. Circle the numbers that are composite numbers:

1	2	3	4	5
6	7	8	9	10
11	12	13	14	15
16	17	18	19	20
21	22	23	24	25

3. Which of the following is a prime number?

A) 6

B) 8

C) 9

D) 11

4. Which of the following is a composite number?

A) 3

B) 5

C) 8

D) 11

5. Which of the following is the smallest prime number?

A) 0

B) 1

C) 2

D) 3

6. Which of the following is not a composite number?

A) 2

B) 4

C) 6

D) 8

American Math Academy

Prime Factorization

Prime Factorization is the form of a number written as the product of its prime factors.

Example: The prime factorization of 96:

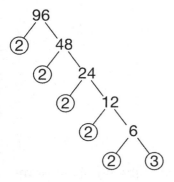

The prime factorization of 96 is $2 \cdot 2 \cdot 2 \cdot 2 \cdot 2 \cdot 3 = 2^5 \cdot 3$

Example: The prime factorization of 108:

The prime factorization of 108 is $2 \cdot 2 \cdot 3 \cdot 3 \cdot 3 = 2^2 \cdot 3^3$

AMERICAN MATH
ACADEMY

Prime Factorization Practice

For questions 1 through 9 complete the factor to find the prime factors of each number.

1)
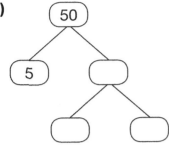

50 = ( ) × ( ) × ( )

2)
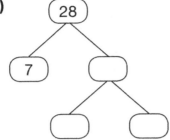

28 = ( ) × ( ) × ( )

3)
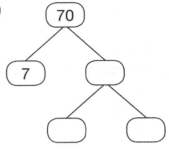

70 = ( ) × ( ) × ( )

4)
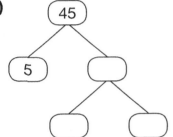

45 = ( ) × ( ) × ( )

5)
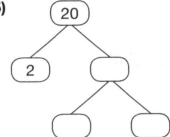

20 = ( ) × ( ) × ( )

6)
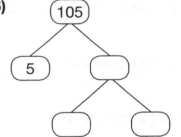

105 = ( ) × ( ) × ( )

7)
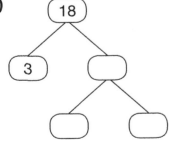

18 = ( ) × ( ) × ( )

8)
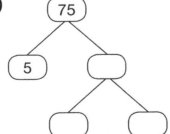

75 = ( ) × ( ) × ( )

9)
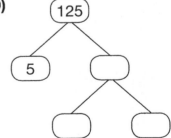

125 = ( ) × ( ) × ( )

Least Common Multiple

Least Common Multiple (LCM): The least common multiple of two numbers is the smallest integer that is a multiple of both numbers.

Example: Find the LCM of 30 and 40.

Solution:

Multiples of 30: 0, 30, 60, 90, **120**, ...

Multiples of 40: 0, 40, 80, **120**, ...

120 are the least common multiple of 30 and 40.

LCM of 30 and 40: **120**

Least Common Multiples Practice

Write the multiples for each pair of numbers. Find the least common multiple (LCM) of each pair of numbers.

1) 15, 45:

    Multiples of 15: _____

    Multiples of 45: _____

    LCM of 15, 45: _____

2) 18, 54:

    Multiples of 18: _____

    Multiples of 54: _____

    LCM of 18, 54 : _____

3) 16, 24:

    Multiples of 16: _____

    Multiples of 24: _____

    LCM of 16, 24: _____

4) 11, 66:

    Multiples of 11: _____

    Multiples of 66: _____

    LCM of 11, 66: _____

5) 10, 15:

    Multiples of 10: _____

    Multiples of 15: _____

    LCM of 10, 15: _____

6) 5, 20:

    Multiples of 5: _____

    Multiples of 20: _____

    LCM of 5, 20 : _____

7) 6, 24:

    Multiples of 6: _____

    Multiples of 24: _____

    LCM of 6, 24: _____

8) 9, 36:

    Multiples of 9: _____

    Multiples of 36: _____

    LCM of 9, 36 : _____

Solving Addition Equations

To solving addition equations step by step:

- Use inverse operations (Inverse operation for adding is subtracting)
- Simplify.
- Check your work.

Examples: Solve the following equations.

1) $x + 6 = 10$

2) $x + 12 = 19$

Solutions:

1) $x + 6 = 10$

$x + 6 - 6 = 10 - 6 \rightarrow$ Subtract 6 from each side.

$x = 4 \rightarrow$ Simplify

Check: $4 + 6 = 10$

$10 = 10$, $x = 4$ is a solution.

2) $x + 12 = 19$

$x + 12 - 12 = 19 - 12 \rightarrow$ Subtract 12 from each side.

$x = 7 \rightarrow$ Simplify

Check: $7 + 12 = 19$

$19 = 19$, $x = 7$ is a solution.

Solving Addition Equations Practice

Solve the following each equations.

1) x + 7 = 13

2) x + 10 = 15

3) x + 25 = 43

4) x + 27 = 55

5) x + 8 = 19

6) x + 18 = 49

7) x + 65 = 88

8) x + 9 = 87

9) x + 81 = 149

10) x + 5 = 98

11) x + 5 = 77

12) x + 41 = 99

13) x + 55 = 105

14) x + 61 = 87

15) x + 18 = 94

16) x + 1.2 = 7.6

17) x + 5 = 10.7

18) x + 4.5 = 23

19) x + 1.10 = 21.5

20) x + 6.1 = 12.3

21) x + 8 = 9.4

22) x + 1.1 = 6.7

23) x + 1.9 = 7.7

24) x + 7.7 = 17.4

Solving Subtraction Equations

To solving subtraction equations step by step:

- Use inverse operations (Inverse operation for subtracting is adding)
- Simplify.
- Check your work.

Examples: Solve the following equations.

1) $x - 7 = 19$

2) $x - 9 = 25$

Solutions:

1) $x - 7 = 19$

$\qquad x - \cancel{7} + \cancel{7} = 19 + 7 \rightarrow$ Add 7 from each side.

$\qquad x = 26 \rightarrow$ Simplify

Check: $26 - 7 = 19$

$19 = 19$, $x = 26$ is a solution.

2) $x - 9 = 25$

$\qquad x - \cancel{9} + \cancel{9} = 25 + 9 \rightarrow$ Add 9 from each side.

$\qquad x = 34 \rightarrow$ Simplify

Check: $34 - 9 = 25$

$25 = 25$, $x = 34$ is a solution.

AMERICAN MATH
ACADEMY

Solving Subtraction Equations Practice

Solve the following each equations.

1) $x - 6 = 14$

2) $x - 10 = 25$

3) $x - 35 = 43$

4) $x - 7 = 54$

5) $x - 11 = 21$

6) $x - 9 = 45$

7) $x - 7 = 8$

8) $x - 9 = 88$

9) $x - 8 = 49$

10) $x - 5 = 98$

11) $x - 5 = 67$

12) $x - 43 = 89$

13) $x - 2.3 = 10.5$

14) $x - 6.1 = 8.7$

15) $x - 1.8 = 9.4$

16) $x - 1.2 = 3.2$

17) $x - 8 = 10.6$

18) $x - 4.3 = 2.0$

19) $x - 1.10 = 2.14$

20) $x - 3.4 = 5.6$

21) $x - 5 = 7.4$

22) $x - 1.1 = 7.7$

23) $x - 1.9 = 4.6$

24) $x - 7 = 3.45$

Solving Multiplication Equations

To solving multiplying equations step by step:

- Use inverse operations (Inverse operation for multiplying is dividing)
- Simplify.
- Check your work.

Examples: Solve the following equations.

1) $2x = 39$

2) $2.1x = 4.2$

Solutions:

1) $2x = 39$

$\dfrac{2x}{2} = \dfrac{39}{2}$ → Divide by 2 each side.

$x = \dfrac{39}{2} = 19.5$ → Simplify

Check: $2 \times 19.5 = 39$

$39 = 39$, $x = 19.5$ is a solution.

2) $2.1x = 4.2$

$\dfrac{2.1x}{2.1} = \dfrac{4.2}{2.1}$ → Divide by 2.1 each side.

$x = \dfrac{4.2}{2.1} = \dfrac{42}{21} = 2$ → Simplify

Check: $2 \times 2.1 = 4.2$

$4.2 = 4.2$, $x = 4.2$ is a solution.

AMERICAN MATH
ACADEMY

Solving Multiplication Equations Practice

Solve the following each equations.

1) $2x = 14$

2) $2x = 25$

3) $5x = 35$

4) $7x = 35$

5) $11x = 44$

6) $3x = 21$

7) $3x = 24$

8) $3x = 36$

9) $4x = 24$

10) $5x = 20$

11) $5x = 45$

12) $10x = 99$

13) $22x = 44$

14) $2.5x = 25$

15) $12x = 96$

16) $3.5x = 70$

17) $10x = 100$

18) $0.5x = 12$

19) $0.2x = 5$

20) $0.3x = 2.4$

21) $6x = 66$

22) $1.1x = 99$

23) $13x = 39$

24) $2.2x = 88$

Solving Division Equations

To solving multiplying equations step by step:

- Cross – multiply
- Simplify.
- Check your work.

Examples: Solve the following equations.

1) $\frac{x}{3} = 7$

2) $\frac{x}{2.5} = 4$

Solutions:

1) $\frac{x}{3} = 7$

$\quad$ $x = 7 \times 3$ Cross–multiply

$\quad$ $x = 3 \times 7$ Simplify

$\quad$ $x = 21$

Check: $\frac{21}{3} = 7$

$7 = 7$, $x = 21$ is a solution.

2) $\frac{x}{2.5} = 4 \rightarrow$ Cross–multiply

$\quad$ $x = 2.5 \times 4 \rightarrow$ Simplify

$\quad$ $x = 10$

Check: $\frac{10}{2.5} = 4$

$4 = 4$, $x = 2.5$ is a solution.

AMERICAN MATH
═ACADEMY═

Solving Division Equations Practice

1) $\dfrac{x}{3} = 14$

2) $\dfrac{x}{2} = 25$

3) $\dfrac{x}{5} = 9$

4) $\dfrac{x}{7} = 5$

5) $\dfrac{x}{11} = 4$

6) $\dfrac{x}{9} = 5$

7) $\dfrac{x}{7} = 8$

8) $\dfrac{x}{9} = 9$

9) $\dfrac{x}{8} = 12$

10) $\dfrac{x}{5} = 13$

11) $\dfrac{x}{6} = 13$

12) $\dfrac{x}{4} = 9$

13) $\dfrac{x}{2.3} = 10$

14) $\dfrac{x}{2.1} = 4$

15) $\dfrac{x}{1.8} = 3$

16) $\dfrac{x}{3.4} = 4$

17) $\dfrac{x}{3.5} = 10$

18) $\dfrac{x}{4.3} = 2$

19) $\dfrac{x}{4} = 5.5$

20) $\dfrac{x}{4} = 2.4$

21) $\dfrac{x}{5} = 5$

22) $\dfrac{x}{1.1} = 9$

23) $\dfrac{x}{1.9} = 3$

24) $\dfrac{x}{7} = 3.4$

1. Which of the following is equal to $7(2 \times 3 - 4) + 14$?

   A) 7

   B) 14

   C) 21

   D) 28

2. Which of following algebraic equations correctly represents this sentence:

   Fifty–five is four times a number, increased by nine.

   A) $55 = 4x - 9$

   B) $55 = 4x + 9$

   C) $9 = 4x - 55$

   D) $9 = 4x + 55$

3. Which of the following number sentences is a correct match with the following sentence:

   14 greater than the product of 5 and 4

   A) $14 + 5 \times 4$

   B) $14 - 5 \times 4$

   C) $5 + 14 \times 4$

   D) $4 + 5 \times 14$

4. Which of the following equations match's the following sentence:

   Subtract 40 from 52 and then divide by 2

   A) $(52 + 2) \div 40$

   B) $(52 + 40) \div 2$

   C) $(52 - 2) \div 40$

   D) $(52 - 40) \div 2$

5. Mr. Johnson gave the following list of numbers to his class. He asked the class to find all of the composite numbers in the list. 3, 4, 7, 11, 14, 19, 21, 33. Which of these shows all of the composite numbers in the list?

   A) 3, 5, 11, 19

   B) 4, 14, 21, 33

   C) 4, 19, 21, 33

   D) 4, 11, 21, 33

6. Which of the following is the smallest prime number?

   A) 0

   B) 1

   C) 2

   D) 3

American Math Academy

7. What is the least common multiple of 5 and 9?

A) 5

B) 9

C) 45

D) 81

10. What are all the factors of 34?

A) 1, 2, 3, 4, 17, 34

B) 0, 2, 3, 17, 34

C) 1, 2, 4, 17, 34

D) 1, 2, 17, 34

8. What is the least common multiple of 5 and 20?

A) 5

B) 10

C) 20

D) 100

11. Which of following is a factor of 39?

A) 2

B) 5

C) 9

D) 13

9. If x is the greatest prime factor of 14 and y is the greatest prime factor of 21, what is the value of x + y?

A) 14

B) 21

C) 35

D) 49

12. Solve: $4 \times 5 - 9$

A) 4

B) 5

C) 10

D) 11

American Math Academy

13. Vera had $75 in her bank account.

She spent $34 of her dollars. How many dollars does she have left in her bank account?

A) $31

B) $34

C) $41

D) $51

15. Solve: $12.3 - 1.22 =$ _____

A) 11.8

B) 11.08

C) 12.8

D) 12.08

14. Solve: $2.3 + 1.25 =$ _____

A) 3.15

B) 3.50

C) 3.55

D) 3.65

16. Solve: $1.3 \times 7.2 =$ _____

A) 6.36

B) 7.36

C) 8.36

D) 9.36

American Math Academy

Customary Units

Customary Units Chart:

Length	Weight	Capacity	Time
1ft(foot) = 12in(inches)	1lb(pound) = 16oz(ounces)	1 gal(gallon) = 4 gt(quart)	1yr = 365 days
1yd(yard) = 3ft(feet)	1ton = 2000lb(pound)	1 qt(quart) = 2 pt(pint)	1hr = 60 minutes
1 yd(yard) = 36 in (inches)		1qt(quart) = 4 cups	1day = 24 hours
1mi(mile) = 5,280ft (feet)		1cup = 8 ounces	1wk = 7days

Example: Convert 4 feet's to inches.

Solution: From chart if 1feet is 12inches, then 4 feet is 4 × 12 = 48 inches.

Examples: Convert 5 yards to inches.

Solution: From chart if 1yard is 36 inches, then 5 yard is 5 × 36 = 180 inches.

Example: Convert 6 pounds into ounces.

Solution: From chart if 1pound is 16 ounces, then 6 pound is 6 × 16 = 96 ounces.

Example: Convert 7 cups into ounces.

Solution: From chart if 1cup is 8 ounces, then 7cup is 7 × 8 = 56 ounces.

Example: Convert 6 hours into minutes.

Solution: From chart if 1hour is 60 minutes, then 6 hours is 6 × 60 = 360 minutes.

Example: Convert 10 days into hours.

Solution: From chart if 1day is 24 hours, then 10 days is 10 × 24 = 240 hours.

Example: Convert 12 weeks into day.

Solution: From chart if 1week is 7 days, then 12 weeks is 12 × 7 = 84 days

Customary Units Practice

1. _____ yards = 12 foots

   A) 1 yard

   B) 2 yards

   C) 3 yards

   D) 4 yards

2. 4 yards = _____ inches

   A) 36 inches

   B) 48 inches

   C) 60 inches

   D) 144 inches

3. 3miles = _____ foots

   A) 5,280 foots

   B) 10,560 foots

   C) 15,840 foots

   D) 21,120 foots

4. 2 pounds = _____ ounces

   A) 8 ounces

   B) 16 ounces

   C) 32 ounces

   D) 48 ounces

5. 5 tons = _____ pounds

   A) 2,000 pounds

   B) 4,000 pounds

   C) 8,000 pounds

   D) 10,000 pounds

American Math Academy

6. 6 cups = _____ ounces

   A) 8 ounces

   B) 24 ounces

   C) 36 ounces

   D) 48 ounces

7. 12 quarts = _____ pints

   A) 12 pints

   B) 24 pints

   C) 36 pints

   D) 48 pints

8. 10 gallons = _____ quarts

   A) 4 quarts

   B) 20 quarts

   C) 40 quarts

   D) 60 quarts

9. 5 years = _____ days

   A) 365 days

   B) 730 days

   C) 1,460 days

   D) 1,825 days

American Math Academy

10. 12 days = _____ hours

   A) 24 hours

   B) 72 hours

   C) 144 hours

   D) 288 hours

Metric Units

Length	Weight	Volume
1km = 1,000m	1kg = 1000g	1 Lt = 1000mL
1m = 100cm	1g = 100cg	1Lt = 100cL
1cm = 10mm	1g = 1,000mg	1mL = 0.001L
1cm = 0.01m	1g = 0.001kg	

Example: Convert 4 km into m.

Solution: From chart if 1 km is 1000m, then 4 km is 4 × 1,000 = 4,000 meters.

Examples: Convert 3 m into cm.

Solution: From chart if 1 m is 100 cm, then 3 m is 3 × 100 = 300 cm.

Example: Convert 9cm into mm.

Solution: From chart if 1cm is 10 mm, then 9 c is 9 × 10 = 90 mm.

Example: Convert 7grams into milligram.

Solution: From chart if 1gram is 1,000mg, then 1g is 7 × 1,000 = 7000 mg.

Example: Convert 600grams into kilogram.

Solution: From chart if 1g is 0.001 kg, then 600g is 600 × 0.001 = 0.6 kg.

Example: Convert 500 milliliters into liter.

Solution: From chart if 1ml is 0.001L, then 500mL is 500 × 0.001 = 0.5 L.

Example: Convert 15 liters into mL.

Solution: From chart if 1L is 1000 mL, then 15 L is 15 × 1,000 = 15,000 mL.

AMERICAN MATH
ACADEMY

Metric Units Practice

1. _____ kg = 10,000g

    A) 1 kg

    B) 5 kg

    C) 8 kg

    D) 10 kg

2. _____ kg = 5,000grams

    A) 0.5 km

    B) 1 km

    C) 5 km

    D) 10 km

3. 100mm = _____ cm

    A) 1 cm

    B) 5 cm

    C) 10 cm

    D) 100 cm

4. 200cm = _____ meters

    A) 0.2 m

    B) 2 m

    C) 20 m

    D) 200 m

5. 5,000mg = _____ grams

    A) 0.5 g

    B) 5 g

    C) 50 g

    D) 500 g

American Math Academy

Metric Units Practice

6. 5m = _____ millimeters

    A) 5 mm

    B) 50 mm

    C) 500 mm

    D) 5,000 mm

7. _____ Liters = 6,000mL

    A) 0.6 Lt

    B) 6 Lt

    C) 60 Lt

    D) 600 Lt

8. 4 liters = _____ milliliters

    A) 40 mL

    B) 400 mL

    C) 4,000 mL

    D) 40,00 mL

9. 4 years = _____ days

    A) 365 days

    B) 730 days

    C) 1,460 days

    D) 1,825 days

10. 8 days = _____ hours

    A) 24 hours

    B) 72 hours

    C) 192 hours

    D) 288 hours

American Math Academy

AMERICAN MATH
—— ACADEMY ——

Volume

Rectangular prism

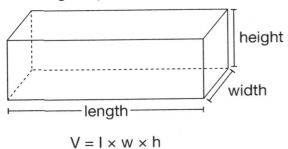

$V = l \times w \times h$

Cube

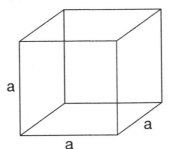

$V = a^3$

Example: what is the volume of following rectangular prism?

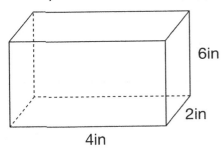

6in

2in

4in

Solution:

Volume = lenth × width × height

$V = l \times w \times h$ l = 4in , w = 2in, and h = 6in

$V = 4in \times 2in \times 6in = 46in^3$

Example: what is the volume of following cube?

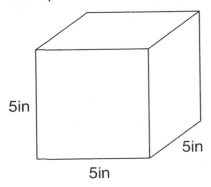

5in

5in

5in

Solution:

Volume = lenth × lenth × lenth = $(lenth)^3$

$V = \neg \times \neg \times \neg$ ¬= 5in, ¬= 5in, and ¬= 5in

$V = 5in \times 5in \times 5in = 125in^3$

Volume Practice

Find the volume of each cube

1. 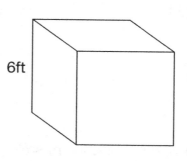 7ft, 7ft, 7ft	**2.** 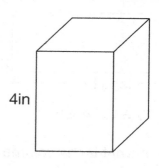 6ft	**3.** 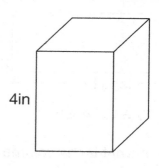 4in
Volume: _____	Volume: _____	Volume: _____

Find the volume of each rectangular prism

4. 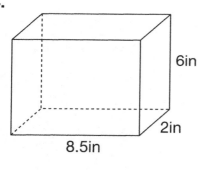 6in, 2in, 8.5in	**5.** 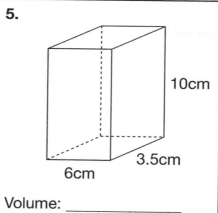 10cm, 3.5cm, 6cm	**6.** 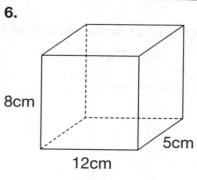 8cm, 5cm, 12cm
Volume: _____	Volume: _____	Volume: _____

AMERICAN MATH
—ACADEMY—

Volume Practice

7. A cube has a volume of 27ft^3. What is the length of one side of the cube?

   A) 1ft

   B) 2ft

   C) 3ft

   D) 4ft

8. A cube has a volume of 125cm^3. What is the length of one side of the cube?

   A) 3cm

   B) 4cm

   C) 5cm

   D) 10cm

9. Find the volume of a rectangular prism that has a length of 3cm, a width of 7cm, and a height of 6.5cm.

   A) 27cm^3

   B) 36.5cm^3

   C) 136cm^3

   D) 136.5cm^3

Chapter 5 Test

1. Which of following is the same length as 1000m?

   A) 1km

   B) 10km

   C) 100km

   D) 1000km

2. Which of following measurement of length is greatest?

   A) 1m

   B) 1cm

   C) 100mm

   D) 1km

3. If the length of classroom is 12 meters. How many cm is that?

   A) 12

   B) 120

   C) 1,200

   D) 12,000

4. _____ Liters = 7,000mL

   A) 0.7

   B) 7

   C) 70

   D) 700

5. 3 years = _____ days

   A) 365

   B) 730

   C) 1,095

   D) 1,825

AMERICAN MATH
ACADEMY

American Math Academy

6. Which one is more, 1000millileters or 2liters?

A) 1000 milliliters

B) 2 liters

C) They are equal

D) None

7. 12 gallons = _____ quarts

A) 4

B) 8

C) 24

D) 48

8. Find the volume of the figure below?

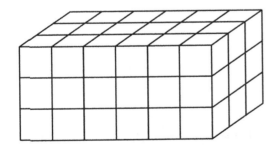

A) 9

B) 27

C) 54

D) 108

9. Find the volume of the figure below?

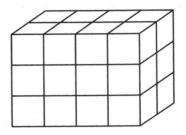

A) 6

B) 9

C) 12

D) 24

10. Find the volume of the figure below?

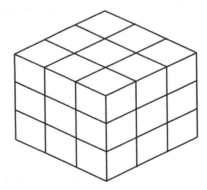

A) 9

B) 27

C) 36

D) 81

Coordinate System

Coordinate System: A coordinate system formed by the intersection of a vertical number line, called the y-axis, and a horizontal number line, called the x-axis.

Origin: A beginning or starting point. The point where lines intersect each other at (0, 0).

Ordered pair: A pair of numbers that can be used to locate a point on a coordinate plane. The order of the numbers in a pair is important, and the x-axis always comes before the y-axis.

Example: (3, 5)

x-coordinate: The first number in an ordered pair is called the x-coordinate.

Example: (4,0)

y-coordinate: The second number in an ordered pair is called the y-coordinate.

Example: (0,7)

Coordinate System Practice

1) List the coordinates for each given point. Give the quadrant for each point.

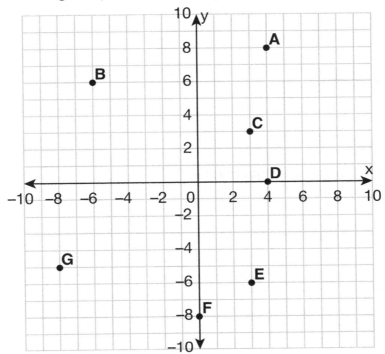

Coordinates	Point	Quadrant
	A	
	B	
	C	
	D	
	E	
	F	
	G	

2) Which ordered pair locates a point on the y-axis?

A) (1, 1)   B) (1, 0)   C) (3, 0)   D) (0, − 1)

3) Which ordered pair locates a point on the x-axis?

A) (3, 1)   B) (4, 0)   C) (3, 6)   D) (0, 8)

4) Which ordered pair located at origin?

A) (5, 2)   B) (7, 0)   C) (3, 0)   D) (0, 0)

Angles

Point: A dot or location.

Point notation: • A or Point A

Line: A line extended forever in both directions.

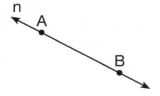

Line notation: Line n or $\overleftrightarrow{AB}$

Line Segment: A part of a line with two endpoints.

A   B

Line Segment

Line segment notation: $\overline{AB}$

Ray: A line that starts at one point and continues on forever in one direction.

A   B

Ray notation: $\overrightarrow{AB}$

AMERICAN MATH
— ACADEMY —

Angles

Parallel Lines: Parallel lines never intersect and stay the same distance apart.

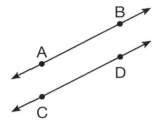

Parallel lines notation: $\overleftrightarrow{AB} \parallel \overleftrightarrow{CD}$

Perpendicular Lines: Perpendicular lines are lines that intersect at a right angle.

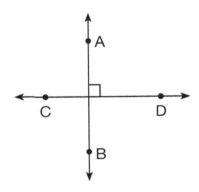

Perpendicular lines notation: $\overleftrightarrow{AB} \perp \overleftrightarrow{CD}$

Intersecting Lines: Intersecting lines are two lines that share exactly one point.

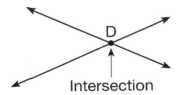

Intersection

Angles

Acute Angle: An angle that is less than 90° but greater than 0°

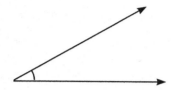

Right Angle: An angle that is exactly 90°

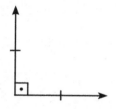

Obtuse Angle: An angle that is greater than 90° but less than 180°

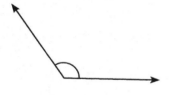

Straight Angle: An angle that is exactly 180°

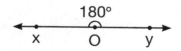

AMERICAN MATH
ACADEMY

Angles Practice

Label each of following angles as acute, obtuse, right or straight.

1)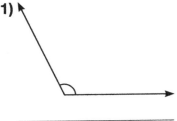

_____

2)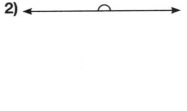

_____

3)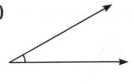

_____

4)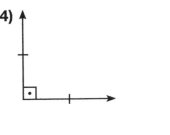

_____

5)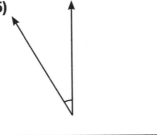

_____

6)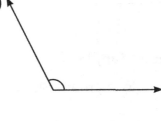

_____

Write line, line segment or ray for each of following lines.

7) A   B

_____

8)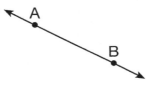

_____

9)

_____

Write Parallel, perpendicular or intersect for each of following lines.

10)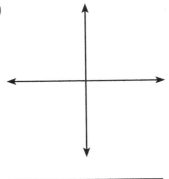

_____

11)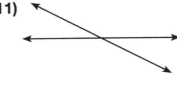

_____

12)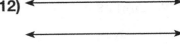

_____

Classifying Triangles

Acute triangle

All angle are less then 90°

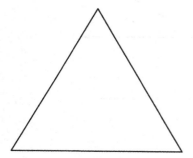

Right triangle

One angle is 90°

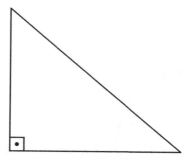

Obtuse triangle

One angle is greater 90° but less than 180°

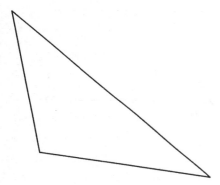

Equilateral triangle

All the three sides are equal.

All the three angles are equal to 60°

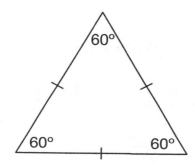

Isosceles triangle

At least any two sides are equal.

Any two angles are equal.

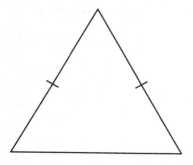

Scalene triangle

All three sides have different lengths.

All three angles are unequal.

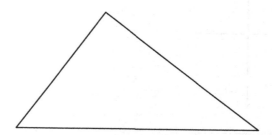

AMERICAN MATH
ACADEMY

Classifying Triangles Practice

Classify each of following triangle as acute, obtuse, equilateral, scalene, or isosceles triangle base on sides.

1)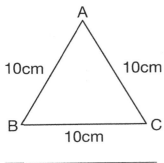

_____

2)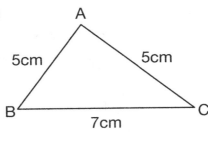

_____

3)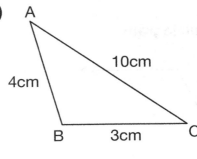

_____

Classify each of following triangle as acute, obtuse, equilateral, scalene, or isosceles triangle base on angles.

4)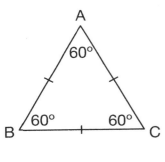

_____

5)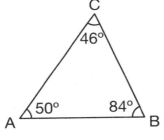

_____

6)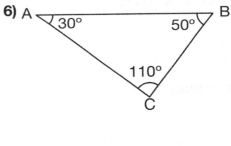

_____

Classify each of following triangle base on angles, and sides.

7)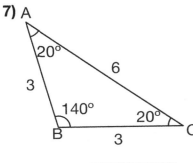

_____

8)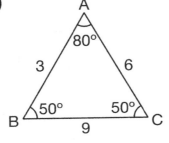

_____

9)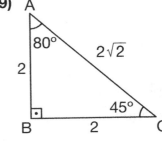

_____

Classifying Quadrilaterals

Quadrilaterals: A quadrilateral is a polygon with four sides and 4 angles.

Parallelogram

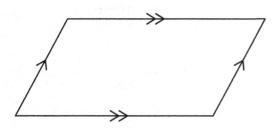

4 sides

4 angles

Opposite sides are parallel

Opposite sides are equal

Rectangle

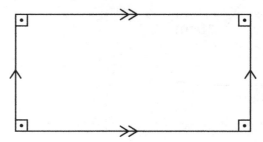

4 sides

4 right angles

Opposite sides are parallel

Opposite sides are equal

Rhombus

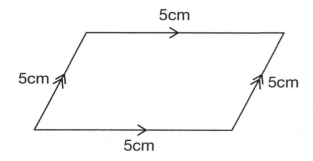

4 sides

4 angles

Opposite sides are parallel

All sides are equal

Square

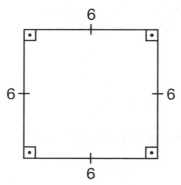

4 sides

4 right angles

Opposite sides are parallel

All sides are equal

AMERICAN MATH
ACADEMY

Classifying Quadrilaterals

Trapezoid

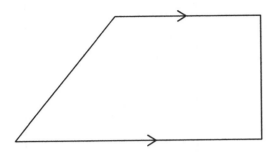

4 sides

4 different angles

Only one pair of sides is parallel

All sides are not equal

Kite

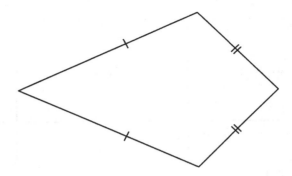

4 sides

4 angles

No parallel sides

2 sides are equal

Classifying Quadrilaterals Practice

Classify each of quadrilaterals from following table.

Grouping	Sides	Angles	Parallel Sides
Rectangle			
Square			
Trapezoid			
Rhombus			
Parallelogram			
Kite			

Area and Perimeter of Polygon

Area and Perimeter of Triangle

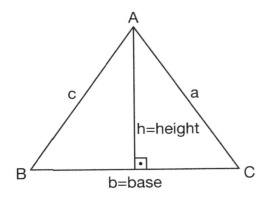

$$\text{Area} = \frac{\text{base} \times \text{hight}}{2}$$

Perimeter = a + b + c

Area and Perimeter of Rectangular

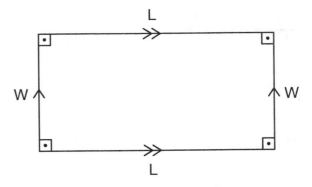

Area = length × width = L × W

Perimeter = 2L + 2W

Example: Find the area and perimeter of triangle below.

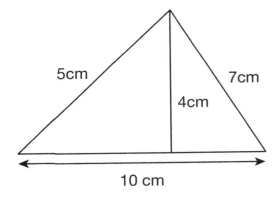

Solution:

$$\text{Area} = \frac{\text{base} \times \text{hight}}{2} = \frac{b \times h}{2} = \frac{4cm \times 10cm}{2} = \frac{40cm^2}{2} = 20cm^2$$

Perimeter = a + b + c = 5cm + 7cm + 10cm = 22cm

Area and Perimeter of Polygon

Example: Find the area and perimeter of rectangular below.

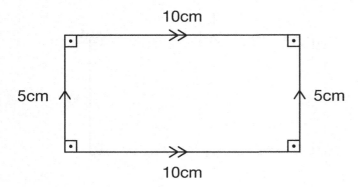

Solution:

Area = length × width = L × W = 5cm × 10cm = 50cm^2

Perimeter = 2L + 2W = 2 × 5cm + 2 × 10cm = 10cm + 20cm = 30cm

Area and Perimeter Practice

Find the perimeter and area of each polygon below.

1)

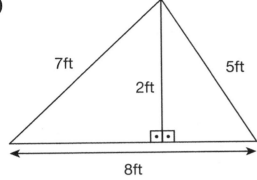

Area: _____ ft^2

Perimeter: _____ ft

2)

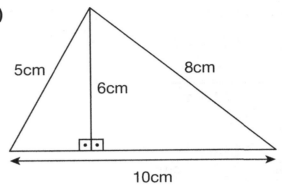

Area: _____ cm^2

Perimeter: _____ cm

3)

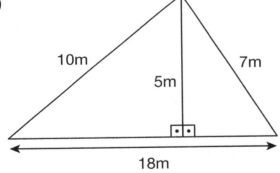

Area: _____ m^2

Perimeter: _____ m

4)

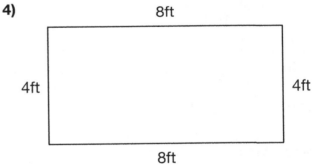

Area: _____ ft^2

Perimeter: _____ ft

Area and Perimeter Practice

5)

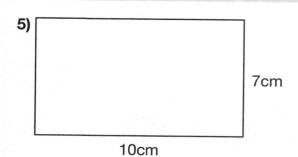

7cm

10cm

Area: _____ cm²

Perimeter: _____ cm

6)

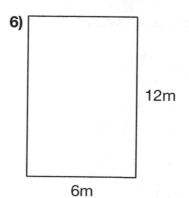

12m

6m

Area: _____ m²

Perimeter: _____ m

7)

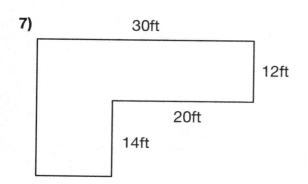

30ft

12ft

20ft

14ft

Area: _____ ft²

Perimeter: _____ ft

8)

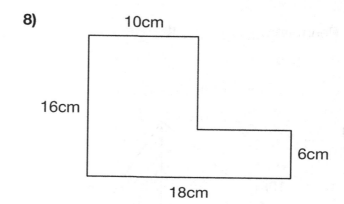

10cm

16cm

6cm

18cm

Area: _____ cm²

Perimeter: _____ cm

9)

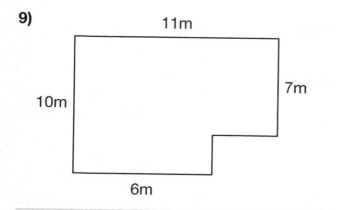

11m

7m

10m

6m

Area: _____ m²

Perimeter: _____ m

AMERICAN MATH
ACADEMY

Circle

Radius: The distance from the center of the circle to the edge.

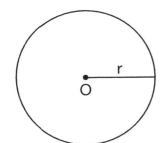

O = center

r = radius

$r = \dfrac{d}{2}$

Chord: A line segment whose endpoints are on the circle.

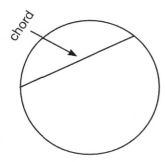

Diameter: A chord that passes through the center of the circle.

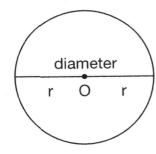

d = diameter

d = 2r

Circumference

$C = \pi d$ or $C = 2\pi r$

Example: Find the radius of circle if d = 10cm?

Solution:

$r = \dfrac{d}{2} = \dfrac{10cm}{2} = 5cm$

Example: Find the diameter of circle if r = 30cm?

Solution:

$d = 2r = 2 \times 30cm = 60cm$

Circle Practice

Find the radius and diameter of each circle?

1)

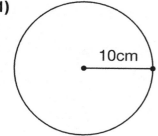

Radius: _____ cm

Diameter: _____ cm

2)

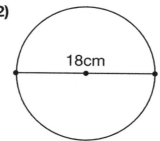

radius: _____ cm

diameter: _____ cm

3)

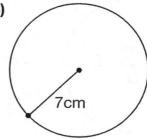

radius: _____ cm

diameter: _____ cm

Find the circumference of each circle. Leave your answer in terms of π. (C = πd or C = 2πr)

4)

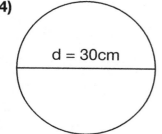

Circumference: _____ πcm

5)

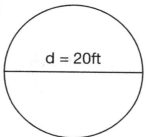

circumference: _____ πft

6)

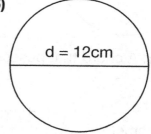

circumference: _____ πcm

Find the diameter and circumference of each circle?

7)

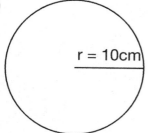

Circumference: _____ πcm

Diameter: _____ cm

8)

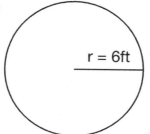

circumference: _____ πft

ptdiameter: _____ ft

9)

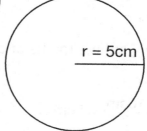

circumference: _____ πcm

diameter: _____ cm

AMERICAN MATH
— ACADEMY —

Chapter 6 Test

1. Find how many cube are in box below?

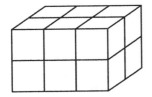

A) 2

B) 4

C) 6

D) 12

2. Find the diameter of circle below.

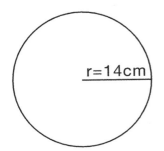

r=14cm

A) 7cm

B) 14cm

C) 12cm

D) 28cm

3. Find how many cube are in box below?

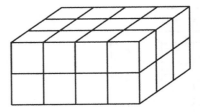

A) 6

B) 9

C) 12

D) 24

4. Find the radius of circle below?

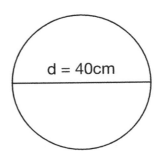

d = 40cm

A) 80cm

B) 40cm

C) 20cm

D) 10cm

American Math Academy

5. Find how many cube are in box below?

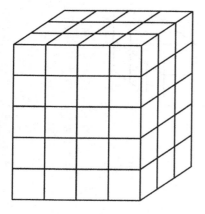

A) 20

B) 40

C) 60

D) 120

6. Find the perimeter of the following shape.

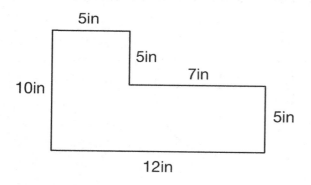

A) 17in

B) 27in

C) 44in

D) 47in

7. Find the area. (The figure is not drawn to scale)

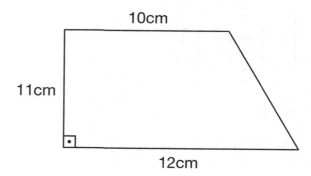

A) 22cm²

B) 44cm²

C) 108cm²

D) 121cm²

8. Find the perimeter of the rectangle.

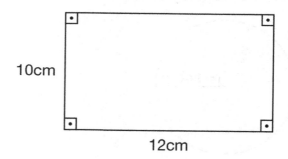

A) 22cm

B) 32cm

C) 44cm

D) 54cm

American Math Academy

9. Which ordered pair locates a point on the y-axis?

A) (3,3)

B) (3,0)

C) (0,3)

D) (0,0)

10. What are the coordinates of point A?

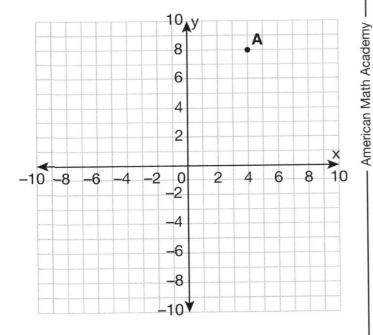

A) (8,4)

B) (4,8)

C) (0,8)

D) (4,0)

11. What type of angle is represented in the diagram?

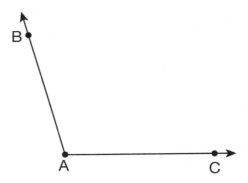

A) Obtuse

B) Acute

C) Right

D) Straight

12. Find x.

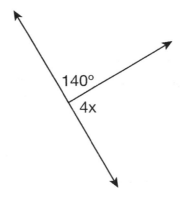

A) 10°

B) 20°

C) 30°

D) 40°

13. Find ∠ABD.

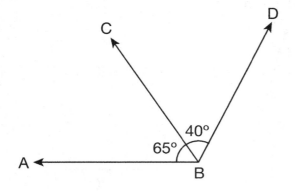

A) 90°

B) 95°

C) 100°

D) 105°

14. Which of following is line segment.

A) •————————→

B) ←————————→

C) •————————•

D) ←————————→

←————————→

15. Which ordered pair located at origin?

A) (0,2)

B) (7,0)

C) (3,5)

D) (0,0)

Mixed Review Test 1

1. What is the value of the digit 6 in the number 6,482?

A) 6

B) 60

C) 600

D) 6,000

2. What is the product of 78 x 66?

A) 5,148

B) 4,181

C) 3,198

D) 2,148

3. Which fraction is equivalent to $\frac{1}{2}$?

A) $\frac{2}{4}$

B) $\frac{3}{6}$

C) $\frac{4}{8}$

D) All of the above

4. What is the perimeter of a rectangle with length 7 units and width 4 units?

A) 11 units

B) 22 units

C) 44 units

D) 28 units

5. What is the value of 125 ÷ 5?

A) 5

B) 25

C) 55

D) 125

6. Which angle is an obtuse angle?

A) 45°

B) 90°

C) 120°

D) 180°

American Math Academy

Mixed Review Test 1

7. A library has 9 shelves with 105 books each. How many books are there in total?

A) 645

B) 745

C) 845

D) 945

8. Which of the following numbers is a prime number?

A) 9

B) 15

C) 21

D) 23

9. Which of the following is the correct expanded form for 3,547?

A) 3,000 + 500 + 40 + 7

B) 300 + 50 + 4 + 7

C) 30 + 5 + 4 + 7

D) 3 + 5 + 4 + 7

10. A box has 5 blue balls, 3 red balls, and 2 green balls. What fraction of the balls are blue?

A) $\frac{1}{2}$

B) $\frac{2}{5}$

C) $\frac{1}{4}$

D) $\frac{1}{10}$

11. Which of the following is NOT a factor of 28?

A) 1

B) 2

C) 7

D) 8

12. A rectangle has an area of 48 square units. If its length is 8 units, what is its width?

A) 5 units

B) 6 units

C) 8 units

D) 10 units

American Math Academy

AMERICAN MATH ACADEMY

Mixed Review Test 1

13. Which number is the smallest?

A) 0.8

B) 0.88

C) 0.888

D) 0.0888

14. Round 678 to the nearest hundred.

A) 600

B) 670

C) 680

D) 700

15. If a candy costs 25 cents, how much do 4 candies cost?

A) 50 cents

B) 75 cents

C) 95 cents

D) 1 dollar

16. Which of these is a composite number?

A) 11

B) 13

C) 17

D) 20

17. Which of the following shapes has more than 4 sides?

A) Triangle

B) Rectangle

C) Pentagon

D) Circle

18. What comes next in the pattern: 4, 9, 16, 25, ...?

A) 30

B) 36

C) 49

D) 64

19. How many faces does a cube have?

A) 4

B) 6

C) 8

D) 12

20. Which of the following is NOT an equivalent fraction of $\frac{1}{2}$?

A) $\frac{5}{10}$

B) $\frac{2}{4}$

C) $\frac{4}{6}$

D) $\frac{3}{6}$

21. What is the missing number? $36 \div ? = 6$

A) 5

B) 6

C) 7

D) 8

22. If the perimeter of a square is 48 units, what is the length of one side?

A) 6 units

B) 12 units

C) 24 units

D) 48 units

23. Subtract: $923 - 687 = ?$

A) 226

B) 236

C) 246

D) 256

24. Sally bought 103 notebooks for $6 each. How much did she spend in total?

A) $518

B) $618

C) $728

D) $838

American Math Academy

Mixed Review Test 2

1. Which of the following numbers is the closest to 1,000 when rounded to the nearest thousand?

A) 849

B) 950

C) 1,049

D) 1,150

2. Which of these fractions is the largest?

A) $\frac{3}{4}$

B) $\frac{5}{6}$

C) $\frac{7}{8}$

D) $\frac{4}{5}$

3. A baker uses $\frac{1}{3}$ cup of sugar for every cookie he bakes. How much sugar does he use for 6 cookies?

A) 1 cup

B) 2 cups

C) 3 cups

D) 6 cups

4. If a rectangle's length is 3 times its width and the perimeter is 32 units, what is the length?

A) 6 units

B) 8 units

C) 10 units

D) 12 units

5. What is the value of $5 \times 5 \times 5$?

A) 10

B) 15

C) 125

D) 150

6. Which of the following is not a multiple of 4?

A) 32

B) 48

C) 60

D) 64

American Math Academy

7. A shirt costs $40 after a 20% discount. What was its original price?

A) $30

B) $48

C) $50

D) $52

10. Which decimal is equivalent to 75%?

A) 0.075

B) 0.75

C) 7.5

D) 75

8. What is the least common multiple (LCM) of 3 and 8?

A) 24

B) 28

C) 36

D) 48

11. What is the prime factorization of 36?

A) 2 x 18

B) 3 x 12

C) 2 x 2 x 3 x 3

D) 3 x 3 x 3 x 3

9. If $\frac{3}{5}$ of a number is 30, what is the number?

A) 20

B) 40

C) 50

D) 60

12. A car travels 60 miles in 1 hour. How long will it take to travel 180 miles at the same speed?

A) 1 hour

B) 2 hours

C) 3 hours

D) 4 hours

American Math Academy

13. What is the missing term in the sequence: 2, 8, 32, ?

A) 64

B) 98

C) 128

D) 156

16. Which fraction is not simplified?

A) $\frac{5}{10}$

B) $\frac{7}{8}$

C) $\frac{3}{4}$

D) $\frac{2}{3}$

14. If a triangle has one angle measuring 90°, what type of triangle is it?

A) Acute

B) Obtuse

C) Right

D) Equilateral

17. What is the next term in the pattern: 5, 10, 20, 40, ...?

A) 45

B) 50

C) 60

D) 80

15. What is the area of a rectangle that has a length of 10 units and a width of 6 units?

A) 40 square units

B) 50 square units

C) 60 square units

D) 70 square units

18. A certain shape has all sides of equal length and four right angles. What shape is it?

A) Square

B) Rectangle

C) Triangle

D) Circle

American Math Academy

19. Which number is NOT divisible by 3?

A) 21

B) 27

C) 34

D) 36

22. Which of the following numbers is a perfect square?

A) 44

B) 50

C) 64

D) 90

20. If you buy 3 identical toys at $15 each and get a fourth one for free, what is the average cost per toy?

A) $10

B) $12.50

C) $15

D) $45

23. Solve for x: $2x + 6 = 14$

A) 3

B) 4

C) 5

D) 6

21. What is the equivalent fraction of $\frac{4}{8}$ when simplified?

A) $\frac{1}{2}$

B) $\frac{3}{4}$

C) $\frac{5}{8}$

D) $\frac{2}{3}$

24. A container has 3.5 liters of water. How many milliliters is this equivalent to?

A) 35

B) 350

C) 3,500

D) 35,000

American Math Academy

Mixed Review Test 3

1. In a box of chocolates, $\frac{1}{4}$ are dark chocolate, and the rest are milk chocolate. If there are 16 dark chocolates, how many chocolates are in the box?

   A) 48

   B) 64

   C) 40

   D) 56

2. If one side of a square measures 9 units, what is the area of the square?

   A) 27 square units

   B) 36 square units

   C) 72 square units

   D) 81 square units

3. In a class, $\frac{2}{5}$ of the students are girls. If there are 12 girls, how many students are in the class?

   A) 15

   B) 20

   C) 25

   D) 30

4. What is the next number in the sequence: 4, 7, 11, 16, ...?

   A) 20

   B) 21

   C) 22

   D) 23

5. Which of these numbers is not a factor of 60?

   A) 2

   B) 7

   C) 10

   D) 12

6. What is the smallest two-digit prime number?

   A) 10

   B) 11

   C) 12

   D) 13

American Math Academy

7. John read $\frac{3}{4}$ of a book. If the book has 80 pages, how many pages has he read?

A) 60

B) 40

C) 50

D) 20

8. The perimeter of a rectangle is 28 units. If the length is 9 units, what is its width?

A) 3 units

B) 5 units

C) 7 units

D) 10 units

9. A bag contains 6 red balls, 4 blue balls, and 10 yellow balls. What fraction of the balls are blue?

A) $\frac{1}{5}$

B) $\frac{2}{5}$

C) $\frac{2}{20}$

D) $\frac{1}{4}$

10. Which of the following decimals is the smallest?

A) 0.9

B) 0.09

C) 0.909

D) 0.099

11. What is the sum of 234 and 567?

A) 701

B) 791

C) 801

D) 901

12. Solve for y: 4y - 7 = 21

A) 6

B) 7

C) 8

D) 9

American Math Academy

Mixed Review Test 3

13. Which of the following shapes has the fewest sides?

A) Pentagon

B) Hexagon

C) Octagon

D) Triangle

16. If 5x = 35, what is x?

A) 5

B) 6

C) 7

D) 8

14. How many vertices does a cube have?

A) 4

B) 6

C) 8

D) 12

17. How many quarters make up $1.50?

A) 4

B) 5

C) 6

D) 8

15. Convert 0.25 to a fraction.

A) $\frac{1}{5}$

B) $\frac{1}{4}$

C) $\frac{2}{5}$

D) $\frac{2}{8}$

18. A shape has 5 sides and 5 vertices. What shape is it?

A) Pentagon

B) Hexagon

C) Octagon

D) Square

American Math Academy

AMERICAN MATH
ACADEMY

131

19. A store sold 250 toys in January and 320 in February. How many toys were sold in total?

A) 540

B) 560

C) 570

D) 580

22. Which of the following is a composite number?

A) 31

B) 37

C) 38

D) 41

20. A car travels at a speed of 50 miles per hour. How far will it go in 4 hours?

A) 150 miles

B) 200 miles

C) 250 miles

D) 300 miles

23. Multiply: 12 x 15 = ?

A) 120

B) 160

C) 170

D) 180

21. Simplify $\frac{7}{14}$.

A) $\frac{1}{7}$

B) $\frac{1}{4}$

C) $\frac{1}{2}$

D) $\frac{3}{4}$

24. If a rectangle has an area of 84 square units and a length of 7 units, what is its width?

A) 7 units

B) 9 units

C) 11 units

D) 12 units

American Math Academy

Mixed Review Test 4

1. How many factors does the number 12 have?

A) 4

B) 5

C) 6

D) 7

2. What is the next number in the series: 5, 10, 20, 40, ...?

A) 60

B) 70

C) 80

D) 100

3. Which of these numbers is a composite number?

A) 13

B) 17

C) 19

D) 21

4. Which fraction is equivalent to 50%?

A) $\frac{1}{3}$

B) $\frac{1}{2}$

C) $\frac{2}{3}$

D) $\frac{3}{4}$

5. How many degrees are in a straight angle?

A) 90°

B) 120°

C) 180°

D) 360°

6. A rectangular garden measures 8 meters by 6 meters. What is its area?

A) 14 sq meters

B) 28 sq meters

C) 48 sq meters

D) 56 sq meters

American Math Academy

7. How many faces does a triangular prism have?

A) 3

B) 4

C) 5

D) 6

10. If a triangle has angles measuring 50°, 70°, and 60°, what kind of triangle is it?

A) Right

B) Acute

C) Obtuse

D) Equilateral

8. What is the value of 85 x 12?

A) 520

B) 870

C) 960

D) 1,020

11. Solve for x: 4x = 32

A) 6

B) 7

C) 8

D) 9

9. Which of the following numbers is the smallest?

A) 0.5

B) 0.05

C) 0.005

D) 0.50

12. What is the quotient of 144 ÷ 12?

A) 12

B) 13

C) 14

D) 15

American Math Academy

Mixed Review Test 4

13. Which number is an even prime?

A) 2

B) 9

C) 15

D) 25

14. If you have 3 apples and cut each into 4 equal parts, how many apple pieces do you have?

A) 6

B) 9

C) 12

D) 15

15. Which of the following numbers is divisible by both 2 and 3?

A) 15

B) 18

C) 21

D) 23

16. A square has a perimeter of 36 units. What is the length of one side?

A) 9 units

B) 12 units

C) 16 units

D) 24 units

17. What is the product of 9 and 8?

A) 17

B) 56

C) 72

D) 81

18. Which of these is NOT a quadrilateral?

A) Square

B) Pentagon

C) Rectangle

D) Parallelogram

19. In a bag of 20 candies, 25% are red. How many candies are red?

A) 4

B) 5

C) 6

D) 8

20. What is the smallest factor of 100 other than 1?

A) 2

B) 4

C) 5

D) 10

21. Which of these numbers is in between 0.1 and 1?

A) 0.01

B) 0.5

C) 1.5

D) 10

22. Convert 0.8 to a fraction.

A) $\frac{4}{5}$

B) $\frac{2}{3}$

C) $\frac{1}{8}$

D) $\frac{6}{10}$

23. If a pizza is divided into 8 equal slices and 5 slices are eaten, what fraction of the pizza remains?

A) $\frac{1}{8}$

B) $\frac{2}{8}$

C) $\frac{3}{8}$

D) $\frac{5}{8}$

24. The difference between a number and 7 is 15. What is the number?

A) 8

B) 9

C) 22

D) 23

American Math Academy

Mixed Review Test 5

1. Which of the following numbers is not a prime number?

A) 2

B) 19

C) 21

D) 23

2. The product of two numbers is 48. If one of the numbers is 6, what is the other number?

A) 7

B) 8

C) 9

D) 12

3. Which fraction is largest?

A) $\frac{2}{5}$

B) $\frac{4}{9}$

C) $\frac{3}{7}$

D) $\frac{5}{11}$

4. If 25% of a number is 50, what is the number?

A) 125

B) 150

C) 200

D) 250

5. Which of the following shapes does not have a right angle?

A) Rectangle

B) Square

C) Circle

D) Right Triangle

6. If a bicycle has 2 wheels, how many wheels do 7 bicycles have?

A) 9

B) 14

C) 16

D) 21

American Math Academy

7. In a pizza parlor, $\frac{2}{8}$ of the pizzas are vegetarian. If there are 16 pizzas, how many are vegetarian?

A) 2

B) 4

C) 6

D) 8

8. What is the smallest three-digit number?

A) 100

B) 101

C) 110

D) 111

9. What is the value of $45 \div 9$?

A) 4

B) 5

C) 6

D) 7

10. How many edges does a cube have?

A) 6

B) 8

C) 10

D) 12

11. Which number completes the pattern: 5, 10, 15, 20, __, 30?

A) 24

B) 25

C) 26

D) 28

12. What is 125 rounded to the nearest ten?

A) 120

B) 123

C) 125

D) 130

American Math Academy

13. If you multiply a number by 0, the product is always:

A) 0

B) 1

C) The same number

D) 10

16. Which number is greater than 5 but less than 9?

A) 4

B) 5

C) 7

D) 10

14. How many minutes are in 3 hours?

A) 90

B) 120

C) 180

D) 360

17. A rectangular prism has how many vertices?

A) 4

B) 6

C) 8

D) 12

15. If the perimeter of a square is 40 units, what is the length of one side?

A) 8 units

B) 10 units

C) 15 units

D) 20 units

18. Which of these numbers is odd?

A) 8

B) 14

C) 22

D) 31

19. What is the difference between the largest and smallest two-digit numbers?

A) 89

B) 90

C) 91

D) 99

20. A parallelogram has how many pairs of parallel sides?

A) 1

B) 2

C) 3

D) 4

21. Solve for x: $3x = 21$

A) 5

B) 6

C) 7

D) 8

22. Convert 0.75 to a fraction.

A) $\frac{1}{2}$

B) $\frac{2}{3}$

C) $\frac{3}{4}$

D) $\frac{4}{5}$

23. Which number is the largest?

A) 0.45

B) 0.5

C) 0.54

D) 0.59

24. If 3 pencils cost 45 cents, how much do 6 pencils cost?

A) 60 cents

B) 75 cents

C) 90 cents

D) 1 dollar

American Math Academy

Final Test

1. What is the value of 4 in 568.473?

   A) 5

   B) 0.4

   C) 0.04

   D) 0.004

2. Which of following decimal has the greatest value?

   A) 24.45

   B) 24.54

   C) 24.60

   D) 24.46

3. Which number rounds to 25,000?

   A) 23,99

   B) 24,098

   C) 24,890

   D) 25,987

4. Round the whole number to the given place 54 to the nearest ten.

   A) 30

   B) 40

   C) 50

   D) 60

5. Which of following expression is the same as 12×10^3?

   A) 12

   B) 120

   C) 1,200

   D) 12,000

6. Which of following expression is the same as 1.4×10^4?

   A) 14

   B) 140

   C) 1,400

   D) 14,000

Final Test

7. Which of following expression is the same as 21.6×10^4?

A) 216

B) 2,160

C) 21,600

D) 216,000

8. Which of following expression is equivalent to 1,000,000?

A) 10^4

B) 10^5

C) 10^6

D) 10^7

9. Which of following can be in the blank to make the statement correct?

45,000 = 45, _____

A) ones

B) tens

C) hundreds

D) thousands

10. $0.213 \times 10^3 =$ _____

A) 2.13

B) 21.3

C) 213

D) 2,130

11. What is 6.12×12?

A) 7.344

B) 73.44

C) 734.4

D) 7,344

12. What is $7.35 - 0.14$?

A) 0.721

B) 7.21

C) 71.2

D) 712

AMERICAN MATH
ACADEMY

American Math Academy

Final Test

13. What is the value of expression below?

1, 237 − 1,198

A) 0.39

B) 3.9

C) 39

D) 390

14. There are 24 students in math class. If $\frac{2}{3}$ of the students in this class are male students, find the number of female students in the math class?

A) 6

B) 8

C) 12

D) 16

15. Which fraction is equivalent to $\frac{1}{3}$?

A) $\frac{15}{2}$

B) $\frac{12}{15}$

C) $\frac{15}{25}$

D) $\frac{5}{15}$

16. Find $1\frac{1}{2} \div 3 = ?$

A) $\frac{1}{2}$

B) $1\frac{1}{2}$

C) $\frac{1}{3}$

D) $\frac{49}{2}$

17. Which of the following is the smallest prime number?

A) 0

B) 1

C) 2

D) 3

18. What is the least common multiple of 5 and 7?

A) 5

B) 7

C) 35

D) 47

American Math Academy

19. What is the least common multiple of 5 and 20?

A) 5

B) 10

C) 20

D) 100

21. If the length of classroom is 8 meters. How many cm is that?

A) 8

B) 80

C) 800

D) 8,000

20. Find how many cube are in box below?

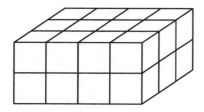

A) 6

B) 9

C) 12

D) 24

22. _____ Liters = 4,000mL

A) 0.4Lt

B) 4Lt

C) 40Lt

D) 400Lt

ANSWER KEYS

Pre-test Answer Key

1	2	3	4	5	6	7	8	9	10	11	12	13	14	15
C	A	D	C	C	C	A	B	B	D	D	D	C	D	C

16	17	18	19	20	21	22	23	24	25	26	27	28	29	30
C	C	C	C	B	C	D	B	C	C	B	B	B	D	C

31	32	33	34	35	36	37	38	39	40	41	42	43	44	45
D	B	B	C	D	B	A	C	D	B	B	C	C	A	A

46	47	48	49	50	51	52	53	54	55	56	57
D	B	B	D	C	C	D	D	C	D	B	C

Expanded Form Whole Numbers Practice Answer Key

1) 9,000,000 + 200,000 + 30,000 + 4,000 + 400 + 50 + 6

2) 7,000,000 + 800,000 + 90,000 + 1,000 + 300 + 40 + 5

3) 800,000 + 40,000 + 5,000 + 600 + 10 + 2

4) 50,000 + 6,000 + 200 + 30 + 1

5) 6,000 + 900 + 10 + 7

6) 200 + 90 + 1

7) 30 + 1

8) 50,000 + 6,000 + 200

9) 6,000 + 900 + 1

10) 50,000 + 800 + 30 + 6

ANSWER KEYS

Expanded Form Decimal Numbers Practice Answer Key

1) 1,000+200+30+5+0.9+0.08

2) 400+80+5+0.1+0.02+0.003

3) 67.108:60+7+0.1+0.08

4) 5+0.1+0.04+0.005

5) 0.9+0.01+0.02

6) 0.01+0.002+0.0006

7) 0.9+0.008+0.0005

8) 1+0.3+0.04+0.005

9) 600+50+4+0.7+0.08+0.009

10) 0.001+0.0005

Standard Form Whole Numbers Practice Answer Key

1) 6,789,914

2) 667,952

3) 9,698,734

4) 87,953

5) 9,498

6) 56,482,345

7) 9,698,731

8) 4,643

9) 919

10) 8,465

11) 461

AMERICAN MATH
ACADEMY

ANSWER KEYS

Standard Form Decimal Numbers Practice Answer Key

1) 679.64

2) 8,374.52

3) 9,738,734.34

4) 0.3976

5) 123.17

6) 5,846,234.53

7) 0.6543

8) 9000.56

9) 900.34

10) 7,400.69

11) 4,622.3

Word Form Whole Numbers Practice Answer Key

1) Seven million seven hundred thirty five thousand, six hundred fourth-five

2) Seven hundred eighty five thousand, one hundred twenty-five

3) Thirty five thousand, five hundred seventy eight

4) Five thousand, nine hundred seventy four

5) Six hundred seventy eight

6) Three thousand, three hundred thirty three

7) Four thousand, four hundred twenty nine

8) Sixty seven thousand, one hundred ninety two

9) Three hundred sixty seven thousand, five hundred seventy four

10) Three thousand, six hundred fourth nine

ANSWER KEYS

Word Form Decimal Numbers Practice Answer Key

1) Four thousand four hundred twenty nine and one tenths

2) Sixty seven thousand, one hundred ninety two and eleven hundredths

3) Five hundred seventy eight thousand, nine hundred thirty two and sixty three hundredths

4) Four hundred sixty five and sixty three hundredths

5) Three hundred fifty four thousandths

6) Eight and nine hundred seventy four thousandths

7) Seven hundred fifty three and seventy eight hundredths

8) Eight thousandths

9) Twelve thousandths

10) Nine hundred eighth seven thousandths

Compering Whole Numbers Practice Answer Key

1	2	3	4	5	6	7	8	9	10	11	12	13	14	15	16	17	18
<	<	>	<	>	<	>	<	<	<	=	=	<	>	<	<	<	>

Compering Decimal Numbers Practice Answer Key

1	2	3	4	5	6	7	8	9	10	11	12	13	14	15	16	17	18
<	<	<	=	<	>	>	>	<	<	<	<	=	<	<	>	=	>

Rounding Whole Numbers Practice Answer Key

1	2	3	4	5	6	7
7,000,000	35,000,000	503,100	7000	2,000,000	380	456,300

8	9	10	11	12	13	14
1,230	3,548,000	12,000,000	130	70	790	890

AMERICAN MATH
ACADEMY

ANSWER KEYS

Rounding Decimal Numbers Practice Answer Key

1	2	3	4	5	6	7	8	9	10	11
33	37	1	7	13	34	71.1	36.4	345.4	56.8	11.6

12	13	14	15	16	17	18	19	20	21	22
64.5	18.69	34.12	5.34	4.479	14.457	74.787	12.568	4.479	1.988	5.346

Powers of Ten Practice Answer Key

1	2	3	4	5	6	7
10^2	10^3	10^4	10^5	10^6	10^9	1,000

8	9	10	11	12	13	14
1,000,000	10,000,000	10	100,000	1,000,000,000	10,000	10,000,000,000

15	16	17	18	19	20	21
1,000,000,000,000	Base: 10 Power: 4	Base: 10 Power: 6	Base: 10 Power: 8	10^4	10^7	10^9

Chapter 1 Test Answer Key

1	2	3	4	5	6	7	8	9	10	11	12	13	14	15	16	17	18	19
C	A	D	C	C	C	D	B	C	B	B	B	D	D	D	D	C	D	C	C

ANSWER KEYS

Adding Whole Numbers Practice Answer Key

1	2	3	4	5	6	7	8	9
11,658	4,721	22,647	328,721	18,200	126,467	3,692	4110	14,772

10	11	12	13	14	15	16	17	18
3,929	3,083	17,853	26,387	328,017	316,387	1,246,014	1,119,492	1,805,008

Adding Decimal Numbers Practice Answer Key

1	2	3	4	5	6	7	8	9
0.15	2.35	14.685	14.665	18.28	126.457	15.97	22.56	269.167

10	11	12	13	14	15	16	17	18
21.62	3.085	14.845	2.877	2.0407	651.189	27.014	126.492	19.2108

Subtracting Whole Numbers Practice Answer Key

1	2	3	4	5	6	7	8	9
951	254	2,043	10,747	7,800	4,667	5,558	90	14,362

10	11	12	13	14	15	16	17	18
829	273	1,437	1,579	19,601	15,587	111,598	850,508	1,550,602

AMERICAN MATH
ACADEMY

ANSWER KEYS

Subtracting Decimal Numbers Practice Answer Key

1	2	3	4	5	6	7	8	9
0.01	0.01	9.39	5.8	4.78	0.087	1.03	0.22	22.033

10	11	12	13	14	15	16	17	18
17.51	3.98	1.19	112.086	0.0353	59.99	41.9	0.508	0.01

Multiplying Whole Numbers Practice Answer Key

1	2	3	4	5	6	7	8	9
375	6,668	3,450	63,858	676	107,730	3,303	35,910	29,520

10	11	12	13	14	15	16	17	18
26,700	274,590	1,260	39,320	63,102	50,000	167,648	492,000	366,415

Multiplying Decimal Numbers Practice Answer Key

1	2	3	4	5	6	7	8	9
12.4	6.88	35	59.2	100	108.3	33.3	171	90.2

10	11	12	13	14	15	16	17	18
11.7	301.5	36	33.2	0.6942	11.25	16.7648	17.204	0.204

ANSWER KEYS

Dividing Whole Numbers Practice Answer Key

1	2	3	4	5	6	7	8	9	10
21	418	69	208	10	27	100	199	12	25

11	12	13	14	15	16	17	18	19	20
41	100	32	60	5	75	30	40	20	21

Dividing Decimal Numbers Practice Answer Key

1	2	3	4	5	6	7	8	9	10
3.2	2.09	0.69	1.04	0.1	50	1.09	0.9	1.2	24

11	12	13	14	15	16	17	18	19	20
4.1	11.1	20	6	14	37.8	3	2	3	6

Adding and Subtracting Patterns Answer Key

1	2	3	4	5
10,13,16,19,22,25	24,34,44,54,64,74	1,6,11,16,21,26	0,6,18,30,42,54	20,29,38,47,56,65

6	7	8	9	10
26,28,30,32,34,36	6,16,26,36,46,56	11,26,34,46,56,66	25,38,50,62,74,76	48,53,58,63,68,73

AMERICAN MATH
ACADEMY

ANSWER KEYS

Multiplication and Division Patterns Answer Key

1	2	3	4	5
21,24,27,30,33	60,65,70,75,80	60,80,100,120,140	36,72,108,144,216	1,3,4,5,6,7

6	7	8	9	10
2,6,10,14,18,20	64,80,96,112,128,144	110,130,150,170,190,210	4,6,8,9,10,11	2,3,4,5,7,9

Chapter 2 Test Answer Key

1	2	3	4	5	6	7	8	9	10	11	12
D	B	B	B	C	C	C	C	B	C	C	C

Fraction and Types of Fractions Practice Answer Key

1	2	3	4	5	6
Proper	Proper	Proper	Improper	Improper	Proper

7	8	9	10	11	12	13
Improper	Proper	Proper	C	D	D	A

Equivalent Fractions Practice Answer Key

1	2	3	4	5	6	7	8	9	10	11	12	13	14	15
2	5	10	7	25	12	50	60	80	4	3	6	B	D	D

Compering Fractions Practice Answer Key

1	2	3	4	5	6	7	8	9	10	11	12	13	14	15	16	17	18
<	>	<	<	>	>	>	>	<	<	>	=	>	=	=	D	A	A

ANSWER KEYS

Adding Likely Fractions Practice Answer Key

1	2	3	4	5	6	7	8	9	10
$5\frac{1}{3}$	$1\frac{7}{10}$	$\frac{15}{19}$	$\frac{3}{4}$	$1\frac{1}{3}$	$2\frac{5}{7}$	$3\frac{2}{11}$	$\frac{9}{10}$	$1\frac{10}{17}$	$\frac{1}{3}$

11	12	13	14	15	16	17	18	19	20	21
$\frac{2}{3}$	$\frac{4}{19}$	$\frac{9}{14}$	$\frac{11}{20}$	$3\frac{16}{17}$	3	6	2	3	$6\frac{2}{5}$	7

Adding Unlike Fractions Practice Answer Key

1	2	3	4	5	6	7	8	9	10
$\frac{11}{15}$	$\frac{9}{20}$	$1\frac{1}{2}$	1	$\frac{14}{15}$	$\frac{7}{27}$	$1\frac{2}{9}$	$\frac{19}{20}$	$\frac{19}{34}$	$1\frac{1}{6}$

11	12	13	14	15	16	17	18	19	20	21
$\frac{14}{15}$	$\frac{4}{9}$	$\frac{5}{14}$	$\frac{3}{8}$	$1\frac{1}{2}$	$\frac{7}{10}$	$\frac{12}{25}$	$1\frac{11}{36}$	$1\frac{5}{18}$	$2\frac{7}{12}$	$2\frac{4}{35}$

Subtracting Likely Fractions Practice Answer Key

1	2	3	4	5	6	7	8	9	10
$2\frac{2}{3}$	$\frac{2}{3}$	$1\frac{13}{19}$	2	1	$\frac{6}{7}$	$\frac{4}{11}$	$2\frac{1}{10}$	$1\frac{13}{17}$	$\frac{4}{15}$

11	12	13	14	15	16	17	18	19	20	21
$\frac{4}{5}$	$3\frac{5}{19}$	$\frac{1}{14}$	$\frac{11}{40}$	1	2	$\frac{9}{10}$	$\frac{1}{3}$	1	2	3

AMERICAN MATH
ACADEMY

ANSWER KEYS

Subtracting Unlikely Fractions Practice Answer Key

1	2	3	4	5	6	7	8	9	10
$\frac{1}{12}$	$\frac{1}{5}$	$\frac{9}{38}$	$2\frac{1}{12}$	$\frac{1}{6}$	$\frac{5}{14}$	$\frac{2}{13}$	$\frac{1}{40}$	$\frac{14}{51}$	$\frac{7}{20}$

11	12	13	14	15	16	17	18	19	20	21
$\frac{5}{6}$	$\frac{1}{3}$	$1\frac{2}{3}$	$\frac{31}{60}$	$\frac{1}{56}$	$2\frac{1}{6}$	$\frac{11}{12}$	$1\frac{1}{3}$	$1\frac{1}{4}$	$2\frac{1}{5}$	$3\frac{17}{24}$

Multiplying Fractions Practice Answer Key

1	2	3	4	5	6	7	8	9	10
$\frac{5}{6}$	$\frac{7}{60}$	$\frac{5}{36}$	$\frac{1}{3}$	$\frac{10}{27}$	$\frac{1}{24}$	$\frac{3}{4}$	$\frac{3}{8}$	5	$\frac{3}{10}$

11	12	13	14	15	16	17	18	19	20	21
4	$\frac{1}{40}$	$3\frac{1}{2}$	$\frac{1}{28}$	2	$\frac{5}{8}$	$1\frac{2}{3}$	$\frac{7}{10}$	$2\frac{2}{3}$	$3\frac{1}{2}$	$10\frac{3}{8}$

Dividing Fractions Practice Answer Key

1	2	3	4	5	6	7	8	9	10
$\frac{3}{25}$	$6\frac{2}{3}$	$\frac{2}{3}$	$\frac{1}{3}$	4	$13\frac{1}{2}$	3	10	1	$\frac{2}{3}$

11	12	13	14	15	16	17	18	19	20	21
1	$\frac{1}{80}$	$\frac{2}{3}$	$\frac{1}{4}$	$1\frac{1}{2}$	1	$\frac{27}{32}$	$2\frac{7}{9}$	$1\frac{7}{8}$	$\frac{13}{19}$	$4\frac{1}{2}$

ANSWER KEYS

Word Problems With Fractions Practice Answer Key

1	2	3	4	5
B	B	B	D	A

Chapter 3 Test Answer Key

1	2	3	4	5	6	7	8	9	10	11	12	13	14	15
D	D	A	A	B	C	A	D	C	D	A	B	B	D	B

Order of Operations Practice Answer Key

1	2	3	4	5	6	7	8	9	10	11	12	13	14	15	16	17	18	19	20	21	22	23	24
2	8	0	0	3	6	9	13	0	−1	8	3	27	13	21	17	17	33	3	0	−3	20	2	32

Prime and Composite Numbers Practice Answer Key

1	2	3	4	5	6
2,3,5,7,11, 13,17,19,23	4,6,8,9,10, 12,14,15,16,18, 20,21,22,24,25	D	C	C	A

AMERICAN MATH
ACADEMY

ANSWER KEYS

Prime Factorization Practice Answer Key

1)
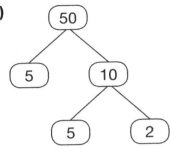

$50 = 5 \times 5 \times 2$

2)
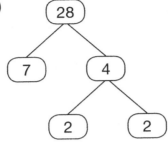

$28 = 7 \times 2 \times 2$

3)
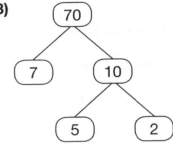

$70 = 7 \times 5 \times 2$

4)
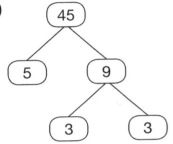

$45 = 5 \times 3 \times 3$

5)
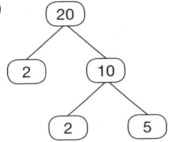

$20 = 2 \times 2 \times 5$

6)
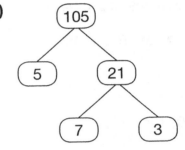

$105 = 5 \times 7 \times 3$

7)
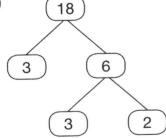

$18 = 3 \times 3 \times 2$

8)
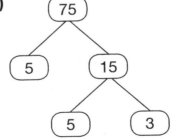

$75 = 5 \times 5 \times 3$

9)
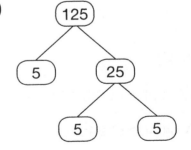

$125 = 5 \times 5 \times 5$

ANSWER KEYS

Least Common Multiplies Practice Answer Key

1) 15, 45:

   1Multiples of 15:15,30,45, …

   Multiples of 45:45,90, …

   LCM of 15, 45:45

2) 18, 54:

   Multiples of 18:18,36,54

   Multiples of 54:54…

   LCM of 18, 54:54…

3) 16, 24:

   Multiples of 16:16,32,48, …

   Multiples of 24:24,48…

   LCM of 16, 24: 48

4) 11,66:

   Multiples of 11:11,22,33,44,55,66, …

   Multiples of 66: 66, …

   LCM of 11, 66:66

5) 10, 15:

   Multiples of 10:10,20,30, …

   Multiples of 15:15,30, …

   LCM of 10,15:30

6) 5, 20:

   Multiples of 5:5,10,15,20, …

   Multiples of 20:20, …

   LCM of 5,20:20

7) 6, 24:

   Multiples of 6:6,12,18,24, …

   Multiples of 24:24, …

   LCM of 6,24:24

8) 9, 36:

   Multiples of 9: 9,18,27,36, …

   Multiples of 36:36, …

   LCM of 9,36:36

AMERICAN MATH
— ACADEMY —

ANSWER KEYS

Solving Addition Equations Practice Answer Key

1	2	3	4	5	6	7	8	9	10	11	12
6	5	18	28	11	31	23	78	68	93	72	58

13	14	15	16	17	18	19	20	21	22	23	24
50	26	80	6.4	5.7	18.5	20.4	6.2	1.4	5.6	5.8	9.7

Solving Subtraction Equations Practice Answer Key

1	2	3	4	5	6	7	8	9	10	11	12
20	35	78	61	32	54	15	97	57	103	72	132

13	14	15	16	17	18	19	20	21	22	23	24
12.8	14.8	11.2	4.4	18.6	6.3	3.24	9	12.4	8.8	6.5	10.45

Solving Multiplication Equations Practice Answer Key

1	2	3	4	5	6	7	8	9	10	11	12
7	12.5	7	5	4	7	8	12	6	4	9	9.9

13	14	15	16	17	18	19	20	21	22	23	24
2	10	8	20	10	24	25	8	11	90	3	40

ANSWER KEYS

Solving Division Equations Practice Answer Key

1	2	3	4	5	6	7	8	9	10	11	12
42	50	45	35	44	45	56	81	96	65	78	36

13	14	15	16	17	18	19	20	21	22	23	24
23	8.4	5.4	13.6	35	8.6	22	9.6	25	9.9	5.7	23.8

Chapter 4 Test Answer Key

1	2	3	4	5	6	7	8	9	10	11	12	13	14	15	16
D	B	A	C	B	C	C	C	A	D	D	D	C	C	B	D

Customary Units Practice Answer Key

1	2	3	4	5	6	7	8	9	10
D	B	C	C	D	D	B	C	D	D

Metric Units Practice Answer Key

1	2	3	4	5	6	7	8	9	10
D	C	C	B	B	D	B	C	C	C

AMERICAN MATH
ACADEMY

ANSWER KEYS

Volume Practice Answer Key

1	2	3	4	5	6	7	8	9
343	216	64	102	210	480	C	C	D

Chapter 5 Test Answer Key

1	2	3	4	5	6	7	8	9	10
A	D	C	B	C	B	D	C	D	B

Coordinate System Practice Answer Key

1		
Coordinates	Point	Quadrant
(4,8)	A	I
(–6,6)	B	II
(3,3)	C	I
(4,0)	D	No quadrant
(3,–6)	E	IV
(0,–8)	F	No quadrant
(–8,–5)	G	III

2	3	4
D	B	D

ANSWER KEYS

Angles Practice Answer Key

1	2	3	4	5	6
Obtuse	Straight	Acute	Right	Acute	Obtuse

7	8	9	10	11	12
Line Segment	Line	Ray	Perpendicular	Intersecting	Parallel

Classifying Triangles Practice Answer Key

1	2	3	4	5	6	7	8	9
Equilateral	Isosceles	Scalene	Equilateral	Acute	Obtuse	Obtuse Isosceles	Acute Scalene	Right Isosceles

Classifying Quadrilaterals Practice Answer Key

Grouping	Sides	Angles	Parallel Sides
Rectangle	4 sides	4 right angles	Opposite sides are parallel
Square	4 sides	4 right angles	Opposite sides are parallel
Trapezoid	4 sides	4 different angles	Only one pair of sides is parallel
Rhombus	4 sides	4 angles	Opposite sides are parallel
Parallelogram	4 sides	4 angles	Opposite sides are parallel
Kite	4 sides	4 angles	No parallel sides

AMERICAN MATH
—ACADEMY—

ANSWER KEYS

Area and Perimeter Practice Answer Key

1	2	3	4	5
Area: 8ft^2 Perimeter: 20ft	Area: 30cm^2 Perimeter: 23ft	Area: 45m^2 Perimeter: 35m	Area: 32ft^2 Perimeter: 24ft	Area: 70cm^2 Perimeter: 34cm

6	7	8	9
Area: 72m^2 Perimeter: 36m	Area: 500ft^2 Perimeter: 112ft	Area: 208cm^2 Perimeter: 68m	Area: 95m^2 Perimeter: 42m

Circle Practice Answer Key

1	2	3	4	5
Radius: 10cm Diameter: 20 cm	Radius: 9cm Diameter: 18cm	Radius: 7cm Diameter: 14cm	Circumference: 30πcm	Circumference: 20πft

6	7	8	9
Circumference: 12πcm	Circumference: 20πcm Diameter: 20cm	Circumference: 12πft Diameter: 12ft	Circumference: 10πcm Diameter: 10cm

Chapter 6 Test Answer Key

1	2	3	4	5	6	7	8	9	10	11	12	13	14	15
D	D	D	C	C	C	D	C	C	B	A	A	D	C	D

Answer Keys

Final Test Answer Key

1	2	3	4	5	6	7	8	9	10	11	12	13	14	15
B	C	C	C	D	D	D	C	D	C	B	B	C	B	D

16	17	18	19	20	21	22
A	C	C	C	D	C	B

Mixed Review Test 1

1	2	3	4	5	6	7	8	9	10	11	12	13	14	15
D	A	D	B	B	C	D	D	A	B	D	B	D	D	D

16	17	18	19	20	21	22	23	24
D	C	B	B	C	A	B	B	B

Mixed Review Test 2

1	2	3	4	5	6	7	8	9	10	11	12	13	14	15
B	C	B	D	C	C	C	A	C	B	C	C	C	C	C

16	17	18	19	20	21	22	23	24
A	D	A	C	B	A	C	B	C

Mixed Review Test 3

1	2	3	4	5	6	7	8	9	10	11	12	13	14	15
B	D	D	D	B	B	A	B	D	B	C	B	D	C	B

16	17	18	19	20	21	22	23	24
C	C	A	C	B	C	C	D	D

Mixed Review Test 4

1	2	3	4	5	6	7	8	9	10	11	12	13	14	15
B	D	D	B	C	C	C	D	C	B	C	A	A	C	B

16	17	18	19	20	21	22	23	24
A	C	B	B	A	B	A	C	C

Mixed Review Test 5

1	2	3	4	5	6	7	8	9	10	11	12	13	14	15
C	B	B	C	C	B	B	A	B	D	B	D	A	C	B

16	17	18	19	20	21	22	23	24
C	C	D	A	B	C	C	D	C

AMERICAN MATH
ACADEMY

NOTE

 **NOTE**

NOTE

Made in the USA
Las Vegas, NV
11 March 2025

19421964R00096